CHENG & TSUI PUBLICATIONS OF RELATED INTEREST

HyperChinese CD ROMs (Macintosh)
by Jing-heng Ma and Robert H. Smitheram

Grammar Modules	0-88727-193-6
Pronunciation Modules	0-88727-223-1

Practical Chinese Reader
Beijing Language Institute, Et. al.

by Ziqiang Shr

by Shou-hsin Teng

Book 1-Traditional	0-88727-229-0
Book 2-Traditional	0-88727-231-2
Book 1-Video Tape	0-88727-162-6
Book 2-Video Tape	0-88727-163-4
Writing Workbook(1&2)	0-88727-191-X

Chinese Unmasked
by Jing-heng Ma

Textbook-Traditional	0-88727-190-1
Textbook-Simplified	0-88727-198-7

Liuxue Shiyong Kouyu: **Studying in China**
by Vivian Ling and James E. Dew

Textbook	0-88727-196-0
Audio Cassettes	0-88727-197-9

Short Chinese TV Plays: An Intermediate Course
by Shou-hsin Teng and Liu Yuehua

Paperback	0-88727-168-5
2 Video Tapes	0-88727-169-3

Taiwan Today, Revised 2nd Edition
by Shou-hsin Teng and Lo Sun Perry

Paperback	0-88727-342-4
Audio Cassettes	0-88727-261-4

A New Text for a Modern China
by Irene Liu and Li Xiaoqi

Textbook	0-88727-312-2
Audio Cassettes	0-88727-383-1

Chinese Breakthrough: Learning Chinese through TV and Newspapers
by Hong Gang Jin, De Bao Xu, and John Berninghausen

Textbook	0-88727-194-4
Audio Cassettes	0-88727-211-8
Video Tape	0-88727-195-2
CD-ROM	0-88727-248-7

Beyond the Basics
by Jianhua Bai, Juyu Sung, and Janet Xhiqun Xing

Textboook	0-88727-226-6
Audio Cassettes	0-88727-250-9

Read Chinese Signs
by Cornelius C. Kubler and Hsiaojung Sharon L. Chi

Institutional Edition	0-88727-182-0
Private Edition	0-88727-183-9

Practical Chinese Reader Companion

Lessons 36-50   Traditional Character Edition   Volume C

實用漢語學習手冊

Practical Chinese Reader Companion

Lessons 36-50   Traditional Character Edition   Volume C

實用漢語學習手冊

Yihua Wang

Cheng & Tsui Company

ABOUT THE AUTHOR

Yihua Wang has been a foreign language educator for over twenty years. She is presently a member of the faculty of the Modern Chinese Language Program at the University of California at Los Angeles.

Practical Chinese Reader series textbooks, writing workbooks, computer software, video tapes, and audio tapes are available from the publisher.

Cheng & Tsui Company
25 West Street
Boston, MA 02111-1213
(800) 554-1963
FAX: (617) 426-3669
http://www.cheng-tsui.com

Library of Congress Catalog Card Number: 96-085849

Practical Chinese Reader Companion, Volume C
Traditional Character Edition ISBN: 0-88727-255-X
Simplified Character Edition ISBN: 0-88727-256-8

Printed in The United States of America

PUBLISHER'S NOTE

The Cheng & Tsui Company is pleased to announce the most recent additions to its Asian Language Series, **Practical Chinese Reader Companion**. This series of workbooks supplements the highly successful introductory Chinese language textbooks, **Practical Chinese Reader, Books I and II**. Designed for beginning students of Mandarin Chinese, the **Practical Chinese Reader** series emphasizes spoken competence through grammar explanations, supplementary reading materials, homework sheets, and other related references.

The **C&T Asian Language Series** is designed to publish and widely distribute quality language texts as they are completed by such leading institutions as the Beijing Language Institute, as well as other significant works in the field of Asian languages developed in the United States and elsewhere.

We welcome readers' comments and suggestions concerning the publications in this series. Please contact the following members of the Editorial Board:

Professor Shou-hsin Teng, Chief Editor
Dept. of Asian Languages and Literature
University of Massachusetts, Amherst, MA 01003

Professor Samuel Cheung
Dept. of East Asian Languages
University of California
Berkeley, CA 94720

Professor Ying-che Li
Dept. of East Asian Languages
University of Hawaii
Honolulu, HI 96822

Professor Timothy Light
Dept. of Religion
Western Michigan University
Kalamazoo, MI 49008

INTRODUCTION

Practical Chinese Reader Companion, Volumes A, B, and C is a series designed to supplement the Beijing Language Institute's **Practical Chinese Reader, Books I and II** (or **PCR I and II**), one of the most widely used elementary Chinese text books at the college level in the United States and elsewhere. All three volumes in the **PCR Companion** series have been used with success for over six years by approximately 1400 students at the University of California, Los Angeles (UCLA).

Because of different school schedules and programs, it is sometimes difficult for schools to finish both **PCR I and II** in a single academic year. **PCR Companion**, therefore, is divided into three volumes to allow for more flexibility and is arranged to correspond with the lessons in **PCR I and II** in the following manner:

PCR Companion	PCR I and II
Volume A	Lessons 1 - 20
Volume B	Lessons 21 - 35
Volume C	Lessons 36 - 50

PCR Companion is available in both a simplified character edition and a traditional character edition. Each volume consists of three parts:

1) **Lecture Notes** help students to preview and review new grammar points introduced in each lesson. Explanations are written with special attention to comparisons between English and Chinese grammar, highlighting common errors made by English-speaking learners. Each presentation of a new sentence pattern is followed by illustrative sentences or mini-dialogs which help students to better understand the pattern and thus enable them to generate their own sentences accurately. In many chapters, interesting supplementary reading texts and exercises are provided to reinforce the new language points presented. In addition to grammar rules, socio-cultural rules are introduced when relevant. Situational dialogs --such as making phone calls, asking for directions, etc.-- are designed for some lessons to provide useful expressions needed in particular circumstances. In order to facilitate teaching and learning, the texts, lists of new words, and lists of characters in some lessons have been edited or replaced by new ones, and the order of presentation of some grammar points have been rearranged. For example, words in **PCR I and II** that are rarely used at the elementary level have been replaced by new, frequently-used words, such as *computer* and *freeway*. Characters newly introduced in each lesson are shown in an enlarged format to ensure that each stroke in the characters is clearly distinguishable.

2) **Homework** is included for every lesson and is designed to test the students' understanding of the language points introduced. Since homework pages in this book are perforated, instructors can ask students to tear out the pages to hand in for evaluation.

3) **Appendices** provide students with some useful references. *Appendix A* contains a key to the exercises in Lessons 36-50. *Appendix B* contains the texts in traditional characters for the corresponding lessons in **PCR I and II**. These are provided for students who wish to learn to read in traditional characters. *Appendix C* contains a glossary index of an edited vocabulary list for **PCR I and II**.

For their insightful comments on the drafts of these books, my thanks go to Eileen Cheng, Xincun Huang, Steve Riep, Hong Zeng, and Ruey-jiuan Wu, who served as Teaching Assistants for the elementary Chinese courses at UCLA. Thanks are also owed to Professor Alan Lamson and the production staff at Cheng & Tsui for their excellent proofreading.

Comments and suggestions are welcomed.

August, 1996

Yihua Wang
wang@ucla.edu
Deptartment of East Asian Languages
UCLA
405 Hilgard Avenue
Los Angeles, CA 90095

CONTENTS

PART I
LECTURE NOTES

LESSON 36

1. Counting to a Billion

The following chart shows the difference between English and Chinese in numeral terms. In Chinese the numeral 萬 stands for ten thousand, and the numeral 億 stands for a hundred million. There are no counterparts in Chinese for the English numerals "million" and "billion," which are expressed by 百萬 (a hundred ten-thousand) and 十億 (ten hundred-million) respectively.

CHINESE	ENGLISH
十 shí	ten
百 bǎi	hundred
千 qiān	thousand
萬 wàn	ten thousand
十萬	hundred thousand
百萬	million
千萬	ten million
億 yì	hundred million
十億	billion

When there is a zero (or several zeroes in a row) in the middle of a figure, the numeral 零 (líng) is inserted.

億				萬	千	百	十		
					6,	7	8	0	六千七百八十
				1	2,	3	0	5	一萬二千三百零五
			5	6	7,	0	8	9	五十六萬七千零八十九
		3,	4	5	0,	0	0	6	三百四十五萬零六
2	5	9,	3	9	0,	0	0	0	二億五千九百三十九萬

3

EXERCISE   Answer the following questions in Chinese:

1.   美國有多少人？   (259,390,000)
       美國有多大？   (3,618,765 平方英里 , píngfāng yīnglǐ,
                              square miles)
2.   中國有多少人？   (1.2 billion)
       中國有多大？   (3,705,386 平方英里)

3.   日本有多少人？   (124,840,000)
       日本有多大？   (145,870 平方英里)

4.   英國有多少人？   (57,960,000)
       英國有多大？   (94,249 平方英里)

2. Money 錢 (qián)
       The following are the measure words for Chinese currency
人民幣 (Renminbi, ¥):

dollar	塊 kuài (in writing: 元 yuán)
dime	毛 máo (in writing: 角 jiǎo)
cent	分 fēn

       In colloquial speech 塊/毛/分 is usually left out at the end of
the figure when there is more than one digit in the figure. When there
is a zero (or several zeroes in a row) in the middle of the figure, a
"零" should be inserted, and in this case 塊/毛/分 is mandatory at
the end of the figure.

¥ 0.05	五分	
¥ 0.10	一毛	xx 十分 xx
¥ 0.25	二毛五 (分)	xx 二十五分 xx
¥ 26.80	二十六塊八 (毛)	
¥ 120.05	一百二十塊零五分	
¥ 475,506.00	四十七萬五千五百零六塊	

* Sentences or phrases marked with xx are ungrammatical.

4

Expressions for asking prices:

- 多少錢？(幾塊？　幾毛？　幾分?)
- 這頂帽子多少錢？　　　　　十五塊六
- 這種郵票多少錢一套？　　　兩塊五(一套　)。
　這種球鞋多少錢一雙？　　　六十九塊九毛九 (一雙)。

3. Ways to Make Comparisons (I)
1) With preposition 比(bǐ)

比 is used to indicate comparison mainly in questions and affirmative sentences.

Declarative	A		比　B　Adj/V(O).
	A	V VOV 得 OV	比　B　Adj/V(O).
Interrogative	A	V VOV 得 OV	比　B　Adj/V(O) 嗎?

- 我同屋比我大，可是他不比我高。 他比我喜歡音樂，歌唱得比我好。以前他中文比我差 。 這次他考試考得比我好。 他現在比以前努力了 。

To negate a sentence with 比 to indicate comparison, add the negative adverb 不 before 比.

– 他不比我高。　　　　　xx 他比我不高。xx

– 他歌唱得不比我好。　xx 他歌唱得比我不好。xx

Degree adverbs 很, 十分 , 非常, 最 can not be used in a sentence with 比 to indicate comparison, but the adverb 更 can.

– 這種碗比那種更便宜。

　　　　　　　　xx 這種碗比那種很便宜。xx

– 他比我更喜歡音樂 。

　　　　　　　　xx 他比我非常喜歡音樂 。 xx

2) With 沒有 (not as......) / 有 (as......as)

沒有／有 are used to indicate comparison mainly in questions and negative sentences. The second syllable of 沒有 is often omitted in negative sentences.

Declarative	A　　　　　　　沒(有) / 有　B　Adj/V(O).		
	A	V VOV 得 O V	沒(有) / 有　B　Adj/V(O).
Interrogative			......　有　　B　Adj/V(O)　嗎? ......　有沒有　B　Adj/V(O)?

A:　你的車有我的車大嗎? /你的車有沒有我的車大?

Is your car as big as mine?

B:　我的車沒(有) 你的大，可是比你的新。

My car is not as big as yours, but it's newer than yours.

A:　你中文説得有沒有我流利 ?/你中文説得有我流利嗎 ?

Do you speak Chinese as fluently as I do?

B:　我沒(有) 你懂中文語法，説得也沒 (有) 你流利，
可是我漢字認識得比你多 。

I don't know Chinese grammar as well as you do, and I don't speak as fluently as you either, but I know more characters than you do.

Notice the difference between 沒有 and 不比:

我的車沒有你的新。 My car is <u>not as new</u> as yours.

我的車不比你的新。 My car is <u>not newer</u> than yours.

3) With adverbs 更 and 最 to show comparative and superlative degrees

更 / 最 + Adj / V

- 我爸爸的車很舊，我哥哥的更舊，我的最舊。

- 我籃球打得不錯 ，我弟弟打得更好。 我們家我哥哥
打得最好。

- 我妹妹最喜歡的電影是 "小美人魚" (The Little Mermaid)，
我弟弟也喜歡 "小美人魚"， 可是他更喜歡 "獅子王"。
(Shīzi Wáng, The Lion King).

4. The Expression "V/Adj + 極了 (jíle, extremely, exceedingly)"

"極了" is used as a complement of degree after a verb or an adjective, meaning "extremely," "exceedingly." It is similar to the expression "太 V/Adj 了."

- 這個電影我喜歡極了。(= 太喜歡了)
- 加州大學隊今天踢得好極了。
- 這輛車貴極了。
- 這條褲子 (kùzi, pants) 長極了！

LEARN CHARACTERS

塊(块)、 毛、 元、 角、 零、 百、 千、
kuài　　　máo　yuán　jiǎo　líng　bǎi　qiān

萬(万)、 共、 種(种)、 套、 便、 宜、
wàn　　　gòng　zhǒng　　tào　pián　yì

貴(贵)、 貨(货)、 極(极)、 只、 碗
guì　　　huò　　　jí　　　zhǐ　　wǎn

* When a character has a simplified version, it is listed in the parentheses.

LESSON 37

GRAMMAR NOTES

l. Ways to Make Comparisons (II)

4) To express similarity with 一樣

Declarative	A　　　　　跟 B （不）一樣　　（+Adj).
	A ｜ V / VOV 得 / OV ｜ 跟 B （不）一樣　（+Adj).
Interrogative	......　一樣　（+Adj）嗎?
	......　一樣不一樣　（+Adj)?

A:　你弟弟跟你一樣高嗎 ？

B:　以前他跟我不一樣高 ，
現在一樣高了 。 以前他
跑得沒有我快 ， 現在
他跑得跟我一樣快了 。

A:　你的自行車跟他的一樣
不一樣 ？

B:　不一樣 。 我的比他的舊 ，
可是我騎得跟他一樣快 。

5)　With complements after the adjective to indicate difference

Declarative	A　　　　比 B Adj ｛ 得多/多了 / 一點兒 /一些 / Numeral + Measure	（big difference） （slight difference） （specific difference）
	A ｜ V / VOV 得 / OV ｜ 比 B Adj ｛ 得多/多了 / 一點兒 /一些 / Numeral + Measure	
Interrogative	......比 B Adj 多少?	

8

高多少?

我比我妹妹高一點兒，
我比我妹妹高一英寸。
我姐姐比我妹妹高得多，
她比我妹妹高一英尺。

我學得比我妹妹努力得多，
可是她考試考得總是比我好一點兒。真氣人！

6) With 早／晚／多／少 as adverbial modifiers before verbs

早／晚／多／少 ＋ V (＋ Numeral ＋ Measure)

- 我比我同屋早起床晚睡覺, 我每天比他少睡三個小時。
  (我同屋比我晚起床早睡覺, 他每天比我多睡三個小時。)

- 大夫説： "你身體不好，應該少喝酒，少吸煙。"

- 這個月我多花了五百塊錢,
  下個月我應該少買東西，少花一點兒錢。

2. Conjunctions "不但 (budan, not only)…, 而且 (erqie, but also)…"

The position of subjects depends on whether the two clauses share the same subject or each clause has its own subject. One of the conjunctions can be omitted when the context is clear.

An optional 也 is often inserted in the 而且 clause. 也 becomes obligatory when 而且 is omitted,.

S1 不但 …, 而且 … (也) …	(one subject)
不但 S1 …, 而且 S2 (也) …	(two subjects)

9

- 中文他不但說得很流利，而且寫得(也)很漂亮。

　中文他說得很流利，而且寫得(也)很漂亮。

　中文他不但說得很流利，寫得也很漂亮。

- 長城上不但中國人很多，而且外國人也很多。

- 這件衣服不但太瘦，而且顏色也不好看。

3. The " 要是 (yàoshi, if)......, 就 (jiù, then)......" Structure

The 要是 clause expresses the premise, condition, while the 就 clause gives a concluding remark. In the 要是 clause, the subject can be placed before or after 要是, but the subject in the 就 clause can only be placed before 就. The conjunction 要是 or the adverb 就 can be omitted when the context is clear.

```
(S) 要是 (S)......, (S) 就......
```

- 要是你喜歡騎自行車，我就送你一輛。

　要是你喜歡喝這種酒，我給你買一瓶。

- 要是有錢，我去中國玩兒一次；沒錢，就不去。

Sometimes the adverb 一定 or 也 is used in the second clause. In that case 就 can be omitted.

- 要是你不再吸煙，我(就)也不再吸煙。

- 要是你去，我(就)一定去。

LEARN CHARACTERS

布、　短、　肥、　瘦、　顏(颜)、　色、　藍(蓝)、
bù　　duǎn　　féi　　shòu　　yán　　　　sè　　lán

灰、　交、　騎(骑)、　尺、　寸、　公、　米、
huī　　jiāo　　qí　　　　chǐ　　cùn　　gōng　　mǐ

*而、　且、　胖
ér　　qiě　　pàng

* Characters listed in the row marked with * are not listed in this lesson in PCR.

10

EXERCISE   Describe the following pictures by making comparisons.

1.

2.

3.

4.

5.

6.

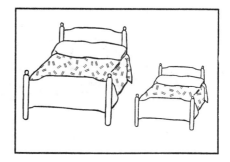

7.

8.

9.

10.

11.

LESSON 38

GRAMMAR NOTES

l. The Resultative Complement

A verb or an adjective which immediately follows the verbal predicate to indicate the result of the action expressed by the verb is a resultative complement.

1. Affirmative: Verbal predicate + V/Adj

聽懂　　　學會　　看見　　飛往　　吃完

回答對　　寫錯　　聽清楚　用壞

2. Interrogative: ...... 嗎?
...... 沒有? (for past actions only)

－ 這個字你常常寫錯嗎?

－ 這個字你以前寫錯過沒有?

3.Negative: 不...... (for habitual /conditional action)
沒(有) ......(for past action only)

－ 我跟他不是一個系的學生，　我不常看見他。

－ 這個字我常常寫錯，　可是昨天考試的時候
　我沒寫錯，我寫對了。

－ 這封信要是今天不寫完，　明天就不能寄。

The verb and its resultative complement are closely linked. If the verb takes an object or an aspect particle 了／過, they are placed **after** the resultative complement.

A: 　你認識古波嗎?

B: 　我聽見過這個名字，　可是沒看見過這個人。

13

A: 喂，這是我的書，你拿錯了。

B: 對不起，我沒看清楚。

The following verbs and adjectives are commonly used as resultative complements:

1) 見 (jiàn, to perceive)   It can be used only after a few verbs. When used after 看 and 聽, it means one has seen something or heard something after the actions "looking at" or "listening to."

    看 to look, watch, read   看見 to catch the sight, to see
    聽 to listen   聽見 to catch the sound, to hear

A: 你看了今天的籃球賽了嗎？看見我了嗎？

    我是五號。

B: 看見了。我大聲地叫："五號加油 (jiā yóu, "Go")!"
    可是你沒聽見。

2) 完 (wán, to complete, finish)

- 語法剛講完，可是課文還沒講完呢。

3) 會 (huì, to master, be able to)

- 這些生詞大家都學會了，可是我還沒學會。

4) 懂 (dǒng, to understand)

- 老師問的問題我沒聽懂，你聽懂了嗎？

5) 往 (wǎng, to go towards)

A: 這輛車開往長城嗎？

B: 不。那輛開往長城。

A: 飛往英國的飛機起飛了嗎？

B: 飛往中國的已經起飛了，飛往英國的還沒有起飛呢。

14

6) 好

    a. same as 完

        – 吃好晚飯我們去看電影吧!

    b. indicates the desired state of an action

        – 我一定要學好中文 。

7) 對 (duì, correct)╱錯(cuo, incorrect)

        – 這個字我沒寫對，左邊寫錯了。

8) 壞 (huài, to break, damage by the action)

        – 對不起，你的照像機我用壞了，我去給你修。

9) 清楚 (qīngchu, clear)

        – 他沒寫清楚，所以我沒看懂。

2. The " 又 Adj/V 又 Adj/V" Structure

This structure is used to indicate that two or more actions, states or qualities exist at the same time.

        – 她穿的襯衫又瘦又長，裙子又短又肥，真難看!
        – 暑假裡他又沒工作，又沒學習，玩兒了三個月。
        – 這輛車又便宜，又好看，又省(shěng, save)
        油 (yóu, gas)。

The words listed after 又 should be of the same category (desirable, not desirable, etc.) Therefore, it is wrong to say:

        xx 這輛車又便宜，又好看，又不省油。 xx
The correct sentence should be:
        - 這輛車又便宜，又好看，可是不省油 。

3. Terms for Asking the Way and Giving Directions

1)   – 請問, 到 (place) 怎麼走?

      坐幾路車？ 在哪兒上車 ／下車／換車 ？

開幾號公路？ 在哪兒上公路 ／下公路？

－ (place) 離這兒遠不遠？ 還有多遠？

還有多少英里? 還有幾站？

2) 往 左／右／東／南／西／北 拐。

3) 從這兒往前走 ／開，到第 (number) 個路口 ／紅綠燈

往(東／南／西／北／左／右)拐。

4) 我沒聽清楚， 請再說一遍。

SUPPLEMENTARY TEXT   補 充 課 文

　　古波和帕蘭卡今天要去丁雲家看她的爸爸媽媽。丁雲家離語言學院不遠， 可是他們不能騎自行車去，因為古波的自行車騎壞了， 還沒修好。

　　帕蘭卡查了查北京地圖， 知道應該先坐 331路公共汽車 ，再換4路電車。丁雲家離4路終點站很近 。

　　公共汽車站在語言學院南邊， 等車的人很多，他們排了十五分鐘的隊才上了車 。買票的時候， 古波問售票員換4路電車在哪兒下車 ， 售票員說: "你們上錯車了 ， 這是往西開的331路。要是想換4路電車， 應該坐開往東邊的，車站在馬路對面。" 他們下了車， 又排了十五分鐘的隊才上對了車 。

　　在4路電車站他們等了二十多分鐘， 過了幾輛4路，可是都沒有停。這時候帕蘭卡看見旁邊有一個牌子，上邊寫 着: "前邊修路， 本站不停車，請在下一站上車 。"

16

他們沒帶地圖，不知道到下一站怎麼走 。一個小學生告訴他們："往前走，在紅綠燈那兒往左拐，過了兩個路口就到了。"古波沒聽懂，他覺得小學生說得又快又不清楚 。他對帕蘭卡說："我們坐出租汽車吧！"他剛說完就看見前邊來了一輛出租汽車 。

NEW WORDS 　生　詞

1.	錯	adj.	cuò	wrong
2.	公共汽車	n.	gōnggòng qìchē	bus
3.	電車	n.	diànchē	trolleybus
4.	出租汽車	n.	chūzū qìchē	taxi
5.	售票員	n.	shòupiàoyuán	ticket seller
6.	站	n.	zhàn	(bus) stop
7.	終點	n.	zhōngdiǎn	(bus) terminal
8.	往	v.	wǎng	to go (to a place)
	往	prep.	wàng	toward, bound for
9.	剛	adv.	gāng	just, a short while ago
10.	換	v.	huàn	to change
11.	東邊	n.	dōngbiān	east
	西邊	n.	xībiān	west
	南邊	n.	nánbiān	south
	北邊	n.	běibiān	north
12.	修	v.	xiū	repair, fix, build
13.	馬路	n.	mǎlù	road, street
	公路	n.	gōnglù	highway, freeway
14.	拐	v.	guǎi	to turn
	拐彎		guǎiwān	to turn
15.	怎麼	pron.	zěnme	how, why

16.	帶	v.	dài	to take, bring
17.	紅綠燈	n.	hónglǜdēng	(red and green) traffic light
18.	路口	n.	lùkǒu	intersection
19.	清楚	adj.	qīngchu	clear
20.	離	prep.	lí	from
21.	排隊		pái duì	to line up
22.	見	v.	jiàn	to perceive (with eyes/ears)
	看見		kànjian	to see, to perceive by the eye
	聽見		tīngjian	to hear, to perceive by the ear
23.	完	v.	wán	to finish, complete
24.	壞	adj.	huài	bad, broken

LEARN CHARACTERS

見(见)、 完、 汽、 剛(刚)、 換(换)、
jiàn   wán   qì   gāng   huàn

南、 終(终)、 彎(弯)、 帶(带)、 跑、
nán   zhōng   wān   dài   pǎo

馬(马)、 爺(爷)、 往、 修、 壞(坏)、
mǎ   yé   wǎng   xiū   huài

*北、 排、 清、 楚
běi   pái   qīng   chǔ

GRAMMAR NOTES

l. Verbs 到, 在, 住, 開 **as Resultative Complements**

1) 到

   a. indicates reaching a certain point or a certain time as a result of an action

   > A:　你們學到第幾課了？

   > B:　我們學到第39課了。

   > A:　要是現在出發，幾點能開到飛機場？

   > B:　十二點一定能開到飛機場。

   > － 昨天晚上我工作到十點。今天早上睡到十點才起床。

   > － 我說到哪兒了？

   b. indicates the attainment of a goal or the successful conclusion of an action.

   > － 運動會上人很多，我沒找到古波。
   > － 我沒買到票，你買到了嗎？
   > － 昨天晚上我不在家，沒有接到他的電話。
   > － 我也聽到了這條新聞。

<--她正在找她的狗。

她找到了。　-->

2) 在 indicates that somebody/something remains in a certain position as a result of an action. It is always followed by a place word.

- 每次上課他都坐在前邊。

- 我住在八號樓，我的車停在三號停車場 (parking lot)。

- 電話號我寫在本子上了，可是本子我放在辦公室 (bàngōngshì, office) 了。

3) 住 indicates that something/somebody is fixed in a certain position as a result of an action.

- 我學過五百多個漢字，可是只記住了三百個。

- 這個球又沒接住，今天五號打得太不好了。

- 你應該留住你爸爸媽媽，

讓他們多住幾天

站住!

別動 (dòng, to move)!

4) 開 indicates that somebody/something is moved away from the original position as a result of an action.

- 走開，我不想跟你說話。

- 請打開書，翻 (fān, to turn) 到第 20頁 (yè, page)。

- 請開開門，教室裡太熱了。

2. The "一 ...... 就 ...... " Structure

1) Indicates the close succession of two actions:

- 我今天一下課就回家了，一回家就睡家了。

2) Indicates a condition and its result:

- 漢字我一學就會，一不複習就忘。

- 為甚麼他總是一上課就想睡覺。

- 一下雨，高速公路 (gāosù gōnglù, freeway)上的車就開得很慢。

The positions of subjects are always before 一 and 就.

3. The Reduplication of Some Adjectives

Some adjectives can be repeated. The repeated adjectives are usually more descriptive, often expressing emotions such as admiration, pleasure, etc. They are followed by 的 when used as attributive modifiers before nouns, and followed by 地 when used as adverbial modifiers before verbs.

l) Monosyllabic adjectives

A	A

– 早早地睡覺 ， 好好地休息

– 黑黑的頭髮， 大大的眼睛，高高的個子

2) Disyllabic adjectives

A A	B B

– 高高興興地跳舞

– 回答得清清楚楚

– 漂漂亮亮的裙子

4. Summary of Particles 呢 and 吧

呢   l) Softens the tone of questions (except for questions ended with 嗎)

  A: 我們坐公共汽車去 ， 怎麼樣?

  B: 坐幾路呢 ? 公共汽車站離這兒遠不遠呢 ?

2) Emphasizes the trueness of a statement, giving a rassuring tone

  A: 別着急，才九點 ， 還早呢 。

  B: 不早了， 晚上我還要複習中文呢 。

3) Indicates a progressive action or a continuous state

  A: 外邊下着雨呢 ， 再坐一會兒吧。

  B: 不坐了， 我朋友正在等我呢 。

4) Helps to form a question

  a. <u>N/Pron/nominal phrase</u> 呢 ? (Where ......? Ask the whereabouts of somebody or something.)

  – 你的飛機票呢 ? 行李呢 ?

b. <u>statement</u> , + <u>N/Pron/nominal phrase</u> 呢？(....., what / how about.....? What the question inquires about depends on the context.)

　　A:　　你叔叔退休了，你阿姨呢？

　　B:　　她還沒有退休。她身體很好，工作得很愉快。

吧　　1) Softens the tone in sentences of request, command, advice or suggestion

　　A:　　不早了，回家吧！

　　B:　　才八點，再玩兒一會兒吧。

2) Indicates estimation, sometimes in the form of a question

　　A:　　那是他鄰居吧？

　　B:　　不是吧，聽說(I hear that) 是一位遠方來的客人　。

3) Indicates agreement after 好, 可以, 行 (xíng, be all right), etc.

　　售貨員：　您穿這件紅顏色的運動衣一定很

　　　　　　　好看，您試一試吧！

　　顧客 (gùkè, customer)：　好吧。

　　A:　　車停在這兒，行嗎？

　　B:　　可以吧，我看沒有問題。

NEW WORDS　　生 詞

(Revised Word List for Lesson 39)

1.	對	prep.	duì	towards, to, for (forms a prepositional phrase to indicate an action towards a person or a place, used as an adverbial adjunct or as a modifier)
2.	關心	v/n.	guānxīn	concern; to show concern for, to be concerned about
3.	阿姨	n.	āyí	auntie (a form of address used by a young person or a child for women about his or her mother's age)
4.	叔叔	n.	shūshu	uncle (a form of address used by a young person or a child for men of his or her father's age but younger)

5.	鄰居	n.	línjū	neighbor
6.	遠方	n.	yuǎnfāng	distant place
7.	客人	n.	kèren	guest
8.	留	v.	liú	to keep, remain; to ask somebody to stay
9.	聰明	adj.	cōngming	smart, bright, clever
10.	不好意思		bù hǎoyìsi	to feel embarrassed; shy; to feel it impolite (to do something)
11.	愉快	adj.	yúkuài	happy, delighted
12.	永遠	adv.	yǒngyuǎn	forever
13.	記	v.	jì	to remember, to keep in mind
14.	本子	n.	běnzi	notebook
15.	運動	n/v.	yùndòng	sports; to do physical exercises
16.	破	adj/v.	pò	to break; broken
17.	跑	v.	pǎo	to run

LEARN CHARACTERS

記 (记)、 永、 關(关)、 句、 阿、 姨、
jì   yǒng   guān   jù   ā   yí

聰(聪)、 叔、 鄰(邻)、 居、
cōng   shū   lín   jū

*運 (运)、 動(动)、 心、 破
yùn   dòng   xīn   pò

LESSONS 41 & 43

GRAMMAR NOTES

The complement of direction is a word or a phrase attached to a verb to indicate the direction towards which an action proceeds.

l. The Simple Complements of Direction 來 and 去

$$\boxed{\text{V} + \text{來/去}}$$

帶來/去，回來/去，進 來/去，出 來/去，過來/去，

送來/去，拿來/去，請來/去，上 來/去，下 來/去，

走來/去，寄 來/去，買 來/去，借來/去，起來， etc.

來/去 does not indicate the actual direction of the action, but the direction in relation to the speaker. 來 is used to indicate a movement which proceeds **towards** the speaker, while 去 is used to indicate a movement which proceeds **away** from the speaker.

> A:　(telephone) 喂，小張在嗎？
>
> B:　不在。他出去了，晚上才回來 。

Rules for positions of the object and the aspect particle 了 in a sentence with complement of direction are as follows:

l) When the object is a place/locality, it is placed **before** 來/去:

$$\boxed{\text{V} + \text{Obj(place/locality)} + \text{來/去}}$$

> A:　星期日你常到哪兒去 ？ xx 星期日你常到去哪兒 ？xx
>
> B:　我常到公園去 。

If the action is completed, the aspect particle 了 should be placed **after** 來/去.

> A:　小張呢? 他回宿舍來了嗎？
>
> B:　沒有。他回家去了。　　　　　　xx 他回了家去。xx

24

來／去.

Habitual or Future Actions	V		+ Obj(person/thing) + 來／去
Past Actions	1)	V + 來／去 + 了 + Obj(person/thing)	
	2)	V	+ 了 + Obj(person/thing) + 來／去

A: 你想帶誰去？　　　xx 你想帶去誰？xx

B: 我想帶我弟弟去。　xx 我想帶去我弟弟。xx

A: 你帶去了甚麼？

B: 我帶了一束花兒去 (or: 我帶去了一束花兒)，她很高興。

A: 他回中國去了沒有？

B: 去年就回去了。已經寄來了三封信了，還寄了一張照片來。

2. The Compound Complements of Direction

The following seven verbs, when combined with the simple complements of direction 來／去, can form thirteen phrases which may function as compound complements of direction.

	上	下	進	出	回	過	起
來	上來	下來	進來	出來	回來	過來	起來
去	上去	下去	進去	出去	回去	過去	

In the compound complement of direction, 來／去 indicates whether the action proceeds towards or away from the speaker, and 上／下／進／出／回／過／起 indicates the actual direction of the action in relation to a place.

站 起來　　坐 下去　　走 進來　　跑 過去　　送 過去

還 回來　　跳 上來　　爬 起來　　買 回來　　寄 出去

拿 出來　　帶 回去　　穿 過去

25

Rules for the positions of the object:

Before 來/去, when the object is a place/locality	拿 上 飛機 來　　　送 進 教室 去 跑 回 家　　來了　　走 過 馬路 去了
Before or after 來/去, when the object is a person/thing	送 過來 一杯牛奶 ／送 過 一杯牛奶　來 帶 回去 那本書了／ 帶 回 那本書　　去 了

PRACTICE　Underline the directional complements in the following passage.

　　一輛車開過來，停在宿舍門口。從車裏走出來了一個新同學。他從車裏拿出來了很多行李。小張從宿舍跑出去，説: "歡迎! 行李我幫你拿進去!" 新同學走進來以後，住在樓上的同學也跑下來跟他説: "歡迎你住進來!"

SUPPLEMENTARY TEXT　　　補 充 課 文

　　考完試以後，古波和帕蘭卡想好好地玩兒玩兒。他們坐公共汽車到北海公園去。司機告訴他們應該在天安門廣場換車。天安門廣場很大，他們花了十分鐘才穿過去，上了開往北海公園的車。車上很擠，因為到北海公園去的人很多。他們正在公園門口排隊買票的時候，看見同學小張走過來了。古波叫他，可是他沒聽見，走進公園去了。

　　公園裏又有山又有水，美極了。古波一看見山就往上爬，一會兒就爬上去了。從山上能看得很遠，北京的建築都看得清清楚楚。他從山上大聲地喊: "帕蘭卡, 你也爬上來吧!" 帕蘭卡説: "我不想上去。這兒有一種黃黃的花兒，真美。你帶照像機來了嗎? 快下來給我照一張!"

　　這時候從旁邊走過來一個人，對帕蘭卡説: "我給你照吧!" 帕蘭卡回過頭來一看，是小張!

```
        *    *    *        *    *    *
```

(下午三點多古波和帕蘭卡才從公園走出來。)

帕:　　　我又餓又渴，你呢？

古:　　　我也有點餓了？看，馬路對面有個飯館
　　　　　我們過去吧。

(在飯館裏)

服務員:　請到前邊去，那兒有空桌子。我一會兒就過去。

古:　　　你累了，快坐下來吧。菜單是中文的，你認識的
　　　　　漢字比我多得多，你點菜吧。

帕:　　　很多字我也不認識。服務員給我們送茶來了，請她
　　　　　給我們介紹介紹吧。

服務員:　我們這兒的小吃比較有名。油餅,炸糕和豆粥都很
　　　　　好吃，豆腐也不錯。

帕:　　　炸糕是甚麼？

服務員:　炸糕是用牛奶，糖，麵和一些別的東西作的。
　　　　　非常好吃。

古:　　　好，來兩碗豆粥，一碗豆腐和四個炸糕。

帕:　　　再來兩個油餅，我們帶回去。

NEW WORDS　生詞

1.	天安門廣場		Tiān'ānmén Guǎngchǎng	Tiananmen Square
2.	穿	v	chuān	to pass through, cross (a square, a street, etc.)
3.	過	v	guò	(of space) to come over, pass by, cross
4.	爬	v	pá	to climb, crawl
5.	一會兒	n	yíhuìr	a little while
6.	建築	n	jiànzhù	building, construction
7.	照像機	n	zhàoxiàngjī	camera
8.	頭	n	tóu	head
9.	出	v	chū	to come out, go out
10.	餓	adj	è	hungry
11.	渴	adj	kě	thirsty
12.	有點兒	adv	yǒudiǎnr	a little (usually used before something unpleasant, undesired)
13.	飯館	n	fànguǎn	restaurant
14.	好吃	adj	hǎochī	delicious, tasty
15.	累	v	lèi	to feel tired
16.	菜單	n	càidān	menu
17.	點菜		diǎn cài	to order dishes (in a restaurant)
18.	小吃	n	xiǎochī	snack, refreshments
19.	比較	adv	bǐjiào	fairly, comparatively
20.	油	n	yóu	oil
21.	餅	n	bǐng	pancake
22.	炸	v	zhá	to fry
23.	糕	n	gāo	cake

28

24.	豆	n	dòu	bean
25.	粥	n	zhōu	porridge
26.	豆腐	n	dòufu	beancurd
27.	牛奶	n	niúnǎi	milk
28.	糖	n	táng	sugar, candy
29.	麵	n	miàn	wheat flour
30.	別的	pron	biéde	other, another
31.	司機	n	sījī	driver
32.	擠	adj	jǐ	crowded
33.	山	n	shān	hill, mountain

EXERCISE 1   Fill in the blanks with directional complements.

1.   我們等了十幾分鐘以後 ， 一位服務員才走 ＿＿＿ 問我們要吃甚麼。

2.   請后邊的同學坐 ＿＿ 前邊 ＿＿。

3.   今天外邊天氣真好, 我們＿＿ ＿＿ 玩兒玩兒吧!

4.   她從錢包 (qiánbāo, purse) 裏拿 ＿＿ ＿＿ 了十塊錢。

5.   前邊車太多了, 我們別開 ＿＿ ＿＿ 了。

6.   小張不在這兒, 他已經回宿舍 ＿＿ 了。

7.   這兒有一把椅子, 坐 ＿＿ ＿＿ 休息一會兒吧!

8.   對不起 ， 我忘了帶照像機 ＿＿ 了, 今天不能照像了。

9.   電影已經開始了, 你們先 ＿＿ ＿＿ 吧。我在外邊等他。

10.   我同屋昨天買 ＿＿ ＿＿ 了一張大桌子。

EXERCISE 2 Describe the following pictures with directional complements:

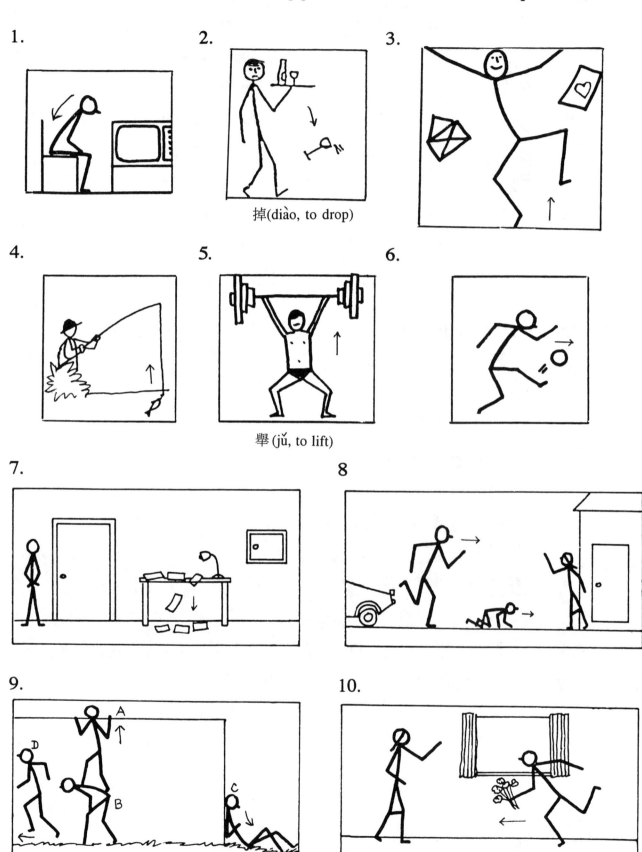

1.

2.

掉(diào, to drop)

3.

4.

5.

舉(jǔ, to lift)

6.

7.

8

9.

10.

11.

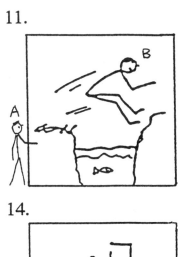

12.

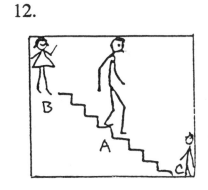

13.

14.

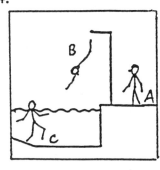

15.

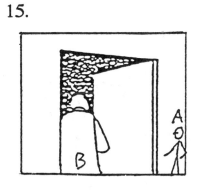

16.

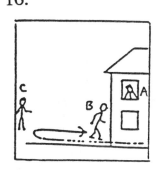

LEARN CHARACTERS

擠(挤)、　司、　建、　築 (筑)、　餓(饿)、
jǐ　　　　sī　　jiàn　　zhù　　　　　è

累、　渴、　糖、　較(较)、　豆、　腐、　粥、
lèi　　kě　　táng　　jiào　　　dòu　　fǔ　　zhōu

糕、　油、　餅(饼)、　牛、　奶、
gāo　　yóu　　bǐng　　　niú　　nǎi

* 廣(广)、　山、
guǎng　　　shān

31

LESSON 42

The Potential Complement

1) In addition to optative verbs 能 and 可以, a potential complement can also express the possibility of an action. The potential complement is formed by inserting the particle 得 between a verb and its resultative or directional complement.

學得好   (can learn well = 能學好)

看得懂   (can understand by reading = 能看懂)

開得過去   (can drive across over there =可以開過去)

A negative potential complement is formed by replacing 得 with 不, and the interrogative form is made by putting together the affirmative form and the negative form or by attaching 嗎 to the affirmative form.

1. Affirmative	V + 得 + resultative/directional complement
2. Negative	V + 不 + resultative/directional complement
3. Interrogative	Affirmative form + Negative form? Affirmative form + 嗎?

A: 　你看得見這些字嗎?　／ 你看得見看不見這些字?

B: 　我看得見上邊的 ， 看不見下邊的 。

2) Although both optative verbs 能/可以 and the potential complement can express possibility, it is more idiomatic in spoken Chinese to use the potential complement when the verb in the sentence is followed by a resultative or a directional complement. Thus, 吃得完, 上得去 are preferred in spoken Chinese to 能吃完, 可以上去. To express impossibility, use the potential complement, because 不能 and 不可以 will be interpreted as prohibition. Compare the following sentences:

－ 不可以進來／ 不能進來 (not allowed to come in)

32

– 進不來 (unable to come in)

3) Word order: The object of the verb is generally placed after the potential complement when it is short, but at the beginning of the sentence when it is long or complicated.

– 我看不懂<u>那本書</u>。

– <u>你去年從中國買回來的那本書</u>我看不懂。

4) Sometimes in the same sentence both an optative verb and an affirmative potential complement are used to strongly emphasize the possibility.

– 你<u>能</u><u>看得懂</u>中文報嗎？

– 這學期我們<u>可以</u><u>學得完</u>這本書。

5) The affirmative form of the potential complement may look the same as that of the complement of degree, but they can be distinguished by the contexts in which they appear.

Complement of degree	Potential complement
你開車開得慢， 你哥哥呢？	那輛舊車他開得快開不快?
他開得快。 (He drives fast.)	他開得快。 (He can drive that old car fast)

6) Verbs 下, 了 and 動 as potential complements

下　　indicates that there is enough room for a certain purpose

– 這輛汽車坐得下五個人嗎？

– 她太餓了，吃得下三碗飯。

了 (liǎo)

　　a. indicates the possibility or ability to perform or realize an action.

– 要是現在出發，下午三點到得了到不了？

– 這個問題太難了，我回答不了。

– 愚公老了，幹不了重活兒了。

33

b. the same as 完(to finish).

　　　－ 我只買一本漢英詞典，用不了五十塊錢。

　　　－ 你們兩個人喝得了喝不了四瓶酒？

動 (dòng) indicates the capability of changing the position of a certain person or thing.

　　　－ 箱子不重，我搬得動。

　　　－ 我太累了，走不動了。

EXERCISE 1 Describe the following pictures. Ask and answer questions using potential complements.

a. Can he drive fast?　　b. Can he get in?　　c. Can he pick up these books?

d. Can he move the desk?　　e. Can she eat the whole loaf?　　f. Can he play basketball today?

 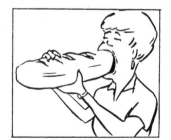 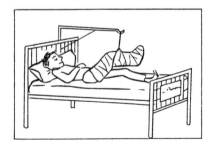

2. Questions with "是不是"

This kind of question is used when the speaker is seeking confirmation. 是不是 can be placed before the predicate, at the beginning of the sentence, or at the end of the sentence. The basic patterns are:

1)		Sub +	是不是 +	Pred +	(Obj)?
2) 是不是 +	Sub			Pred +	(Obj)?
3)	Sub			Pred +	(Obj), 是不是 ?

– 現在學中文的人是不是很多 ？

– 你們是不是學完第四十二課了 ？

– 是不是應該在天安門廣場換車 ？

– 那座山你爬上去過 ， 是不是 ？

When the main verb of the sentence is 是 , do not use this question form; use the affirmative-negative question form instead.

– 她是不是中國留學生 ？

            xx 她是不是是中國留學生 ? xx

NEW WORDS   生 詞

(for the text of 愚公移山 Yúgōng yí shān, page 300, PCR Book II)

1.	移	v	yí	to remove, to move
2.	古時候	n	gǔshíhou	ancient times
3.	座	m	zuò	a measure word for 牆, 山, etc.
4.	方便	adj	fāngbian	convenient
5.	搬	v	bān	to move, to take away
6.	兒子	n	érzi	son
7.	孫子	n	sūnzi	grandson
8.	妻子	n	qīzi	wife
9.	幹	v	gàn	to work, to do

10.	這麼	pron	zhème	so, such, like this (used to modify a verb or an adjective to express special quality, state, manner or degree)
11.	石頭	n	shítou	stone, rock
12.	動	v	dòng	to move
13.	了	v	liǎo	(to indicate possibility/finality when used as a potential complement)
14.	海	n	hǎi	sea
15.	聽說		tīng shuō	It is said that..., I hear that...
16.	怕	v	pà	to fear, be afraid of
17.	不停地		bùtíngde	continuously
18.	可笑	adj	kěxiào	ridiculous, laughable
19.	歲數	n	suìshu	age
20.	死	v	sǐ	to die
21.	重	adj	zhòng	heavy
22.	活兒	n	huór	work, job

LEARN CHARACTERS:

搬、 座、 石、 海、 孫 (孙)、 怕
bān　　zuò　　shí　　hǎi　　sūn　　　　pà

數 (数)、 重、 活、 幹 (干)、 妻、
shù　　　　zhòng　huó　　gàn　　　　qī

動 (动)、 死、
dòng　　　　sǐ

EXERCISE 2   Fill in the following blanks with complements:

1. - 你記 ＿＿ 他的地址了嗎?

    - 我記 ＿＿ 本子上了, 可是我沒找 ＿＿ 那個本子。

2. - 請打 ＿＿ 書, 翻 ＿＿ 第四十四課。

    - 老師, 第四十三課我們還沒學 ＿＿ 呢!

3. - 小張呢? 這是他忘 ＿＿ 教室裏的毛衣, 我給他帶 ＿＿ 了。

    - 他還沒從學校回 ＿＿ 呢。你放 ＿＿ 他的床上吧。

4. 搬 ＿＿ 這張桌子, 拿＿＿ 那些椅子! 我買 ＿＿ ＿＿ 了一張大床,
    要放 ＿＿ 這兒。

5. 司機在外邊等你, 你快出 ＿＿ 吧。行李我已經給你拿 ＿＿ ＿＿ 了。

6. 這個小山我已經爬 ＿＿ ＿＿ 過兩次了。上 ＿＿ 容易, 下＿＿ 難。

7. - 百貨大樓在馬路對面, 我們過 ＿＿ 吧。

    - 這兒不能過馬路, 應該從路口那兒走＿＿ ＿＿。

8. 我阿姨給我寄 ＿＿ 了一個新式照像機, 可是我還沒學 ＿＿
    怎麼用呢。

9. PIZZA 店的服務員給我送 ＿＿ 了一個 PIZZA 餅。我剛吃 ＿＿ ,
    他又回 ＿＿ 了, 他説他送 ＿＿ 了, 那是我鄰居買的。

10. 對不起, 我沒聽＿＿ ＿＿, 請再説一遍。

11. 這座牆不高, 我能爬＿＿ ＿＿。你呢? 爬＿＿ ＿＿ ＿＿ 嗎?

12. 你的車坐 ＿＿ ＿＿坐＿＿ ＿＿五個人?

13. 你一星期記 ＿＿ ＿＿記＿＿ ＿＿一百個生詞?

14. 坐＿＿ 教室後邊的同學聽＿＿ 清楚老師説的話嗎?

15. 一聽 ＿＿ 這個新聞, 小張就高興得跳 ＿＿ ＿＿ 了。

37

LESSON 44

1. The "是 ...... 的" Structure

This structure is used in a sentence to emphasize the time, place, manner, purpose, origin, beneficiary, etc. of an action which took place in the past. "是" is not the predicate verb in such a sentence.

Question:	是 ...... V (O) 的嗎?
Affirmative:	是 ...... V (O) 的
negative:	不是 ...... V (O) 的

"是" is placed immediately before the word/word group to be emphasized. It can sometimes be omitted.

A:　　你的中文不錯，(是)在哪兒學的？

B:　　(是)在北京學的。

PRACTICE　　　Answer the following questions according to the information given.

　　　小張一九七八年生在美國加州。昨天他跟他姐姐一起去北京了。他們去北京大學學中文。他們中午坐日本飛機從洛杉磯國際機場起飛，到北京的時候是昨天上午。

－ 小張是哪年生的？是在哪兒生的？

－ 他是跟誰一起去北京的？

－ 他們是去玩兒的嗎？

－ 他們是坐哪國飛機去的？

－ 他們的飛機是從哪個機場起飛的？

－ 他們是甚麼時候到北京的？

"的" usually comes at the end of the sentence, but when the verb in

38

the sentence takes a non-pronoun object, "的" can also be placed before the object.

- 我是去年九月開始學的中文。

  (= 我是去年九月開始學中文的。)

- 我是上星期看見她的 。 xx 我是上星期看見的她 。 xx

In the following sentences, "是" is the predicate verb. These sentences end with a "的", because the nouns after "的" are omitted. These are **NOT** sentences of "是……的" structure.

- 那些搬山的人是愚公家的 (人)嗎？

- 那個故事不是新的 (故事)。

- 這座橋是中國式的(橋)。

PRACTICE Ask and answer questions about the underlined parts, using "是……的" structure.

古波的母親昨天晚上從美國打電話來了，可是古波不在宿舍。

他跟帕蘭卡騎自行車到一家新飯館去吃晚飯了 。

2. The "只有……, 才……" Structure

The connective 只有 introduces a necessary condition, while the adverb 才(which is often followed by optative verbs 能, 會, 可以, etc.) introduces the result. If there is only one subject in this structure, it should be placed before 只有 or 才. If each clause has a different subject, Subject 1 should be placed after 只有 and Sub 2 should be before 才. 只有 can be omitted.

1)	只有……, S1才…… or S1 只有……, 才……
2)	只有 S1 ……, S2 才……

- 只有 七點以前起床，你八點才能到學校。

  (= 你只有七點以前起床， 八點才能到學校。)

- (只有)天氣好，我才能去長城。

- (只有)天天練習才寫得好漢字。

3. The Exclamatory Structure "多(麼) + Adj/V + 啊!"

Like the "太 Adj/V 了" and "Adj/V 極了" structures introduced previously, this structure is also used in exclamatory sentences expressing a high degree of emotion.

> – 湖上的船多麼漂亮啊！

> – 我多想早一點兒畢業啊！

> – 加州的天氣多麼好啊！ 我多喜歡住在加州啊！

> – 他寫的字多難看啊！

4. Verb Phrases as Complements of Degree
In addition to adjectives, verb phrases can also be used as complements of degree.

> – 我累得走不動了。

> – 她高興得跳起來了。

> – 昨天我忙得沒吃晚飯， 只睡了四個小時。

5. "一天比一天 " and "一年比一年 "
These phrases are used as adverbials to indicate the continuous changes that accompany the passing of time.

> – 學中文的學生一年比一年多。

> – 學費 (xuéfèi, tuition) 一年比一年貴了。

> – 天氣一天比一天熱了。

LEARN CHARACTERS

決、 貿(贸)、 喊、 旅、 它、 母、
jué   mào   hǎn   lǚ   tā   mǔ

親(亲)、 湖 、 爬、 橋(桥)、 船、
qīn   hú   pá   qiáo   chuán

草、 幅、 陽(阳)、 畢(毕)、 業(业)、
cǎo   fú   yáng   bì   yè

*父
fù

40

LESSONS 46 & 47

GRAMMAR NOTES

I. The 把-sentence

      The 把-sentence is frequently found in daily speech. It expresses how a thing/person is disposed of, dealt with, or affected by the action expressed by the verb. The preposition 把 also makes the object of the predicate verb a focal point by preposing it before the verb. Compare the following dialogs to see the difference in meaning between a sentence with a regular word order and a 把-sentence:

1) – 下午你幹甚麼了？ (What did you do in the afternoon?)

    – 我洗衣服了。 (I did laundry.)

2) – 衣服呢？ (Where are the clothes?)

    – 我把衣服洗了。 (I already washed them.)

The basic sentence pattern is:

Subject (Doer of the action)	Adverbial	把 + Object	Transitive Verb (which can affect the obj.)	Other Element(s)
我同屋	昨天	把 他的車	開	壞了。
他	沒有	把 錄音機	還	我。
護士	也	把 藥	拿	來了。
我		把 錢	花	了。
你	應該	把 衣服	洗	洗。
老師		把 語法	講	得很清楚。
你		把 窗戶	打	開!
		把 電視機	關	上！

Since the object of a 把-sentence is to be disposed of, it usually represents something (or somebody) specific.

41

Rules for 把-sentences:

l. The predicate verb must be a **transitive** verb and also a verb that can govern or influence the object. Therefore verbs such as 有, 在, 是, 知道, 認識, 住, 喜歡, 開始, 去, 來, 坐, 睡 can't be used as the predicate verbs in 把-sentences.

2. The predicate verb must be followed by some other elements. The "other elements" can be a complement (except potential complement), an indirect object, a particle or a reduplicated verb.

3. The preposition 把 can have before it an adverbial adjunct, such as a time word, optative verb, adverb, etc.

4. Some predicate verbs are followed by complicated constructions, thus the objects should be preposed before the verbs to avoid too many elements clustering after the verb. In this case, the 把-sentence should be used, and the regular "S-V-O" word order is considered ungrammatical. These verb constructions are:

1) V	+ resultative compl.	到/在 成 給	+ Obj(place/locality) + Obj (result) + Obj (recipient)

－ 我沒把車開到門口。我把車停在馬路對面了。

    xx 我沒開車到門口。我停車在馬路對面了。xx

－ 請把藥放在桌子上。   xx 請放藥在桌子上。xx

－ 我常常把"已經" 寫成 "己經 "。

    xx 我常常寫"已經"成 "己經 "。xx

－ 你把作業 (zuòyè, homework) 交給老師了嗎?

    xx 你交作業給老師了嗎 ? xx

2) V	+ compound directional compl.	+ Obj (place/locality)

－ 你把行李搬上樓去吧 。   xx 你搬行李上樓去吧！xx

－ 我們把書拿進教室來吧。xx 我們拿書進教室來。xx

2. The "除了⋯⋯（以外）" Structure

1) When followed by adverbs 也／還, it means "in addition to":

　　　- 除了中文以外， 我也會說日文和法文。

　　　- 除了咳嗽以外， 她還頭疼和發燒 。

　　　- 除了中國， 你也去過日本嗎?

2) When followed by adverbs 都／沒有, it means "except":

　　　- 除了藥以外， 桌子上沒有別的東西 。

　　　- 我們班除了小張學日文， 別人都學中文 。

"以外" can be omitted.

SUPPLEMENTARY TEXT　　　　　補 充 課 文

　　帕蘭卡已經病了兩天了。 她覺得很不舒服， 頭疼得很厲害 ， 吃不下東西 ， 而且又咳嗽又發燒 。 昨天下午古波開車把她送到醫院去了。 內科大夫檢查了以後, 對帕蘭卡說: "你得了重感冒， 要立刻住院。" 護士把她送進內科病房以後給她打了針， 還讓她把大夫開的藥吃下去。 那種藥每天要吃六次， 每次一片 。

　　晚上古波又回到醫院去， 帶去了一束花兒 ， 一個錄音機和很多錄音帶 。 錄音帶上除了西方音樂以外 ， 還有很多好聽的中國民歌。 他還帶去了帕蘭卡喜歡吃的炸糕。 護士對他說: " 太晚了， 你不能進病房去了, 病人已經睡覺了。 " 她還說: " 除了炸糕以外， 別的都可以留下來。 我會把這些東西送到她的病房去 。 "

　　古波很着急 ， 今天早上一起床就去醫院了 。 帕蘭卡正躺着聽音樂呢。 她一看見古波就把錄音機關上 ， 高興地說: "我好多了! 護士剛給我量了體溫， 已經不發燒了。 " 古波笑着説: "太好了。這幾天天氣不好，得病的人很多。我們班上除了你以外，小張和小李也感冒了。"

NEW WORDS 生 詞

1.	把	prep.	bǎ	*a preposition*
2.	病	n&v	bìng	to be ill, illness
3.	病房	n	bìngfáng	ward (of a hospital)
4.	病人	n	bìngrén	patient
5.	舒服	adj	shūfu	comfortable, well
6.	頭	n	tóu	head
7.	疼	adj	téng	ache, pain, sore
8.	厲害	adj	lìhai	serious, terrible
9.	咳嗽	v	késou	to cough
10.	發燒		fā shāo	to have a fever
11.	內科	n	nèikē	department of internal medicine
12.	感冒	v&n	gǎnmào	to catch a cold; cold
13.	住院		zhù yuàn	to be hospitalized
14.	護士	n	hùshi	nurse
15.	打針		dǎ zhēn	to give or have an injection
16.	針	n	zhēn	injection, needle
17.	藥	n	yào	medicine
18.	開藥		kāi yào	to write out a prescription
19.	片	m	piàn	tablet, slice, etc.
20.	錄音機	n	lùyīnjī	tape-recorder

21.	錄音帶	n	lùyīndài	audio-tape
22.	除了	prep	chúle	in addition to, except (often used together with 以外）
23.	躺	v	tǎng	to lie (on one's back or side)
24.	量	v	liáng	to measure
25.	體溫	n	tǐwēn	(body) temperature
26.	立刻	adv	lìkè	immediately
27.	得	v	dé	to get, obtain
28.	關	v	guān	to close, shut, turn off

LEARN CHARACTERS

把、 藥(药)、 疼、 舒、 躺、 燒(烧)、
bǎ   yào   téng   shū   tǎng   shāo

厲(厉)、 害、 冒、 針(针)、 温、 度、
lì   hài   mào   zhēn   wēn   dù

*除、 錄(录)、 片、 内、 科、 感、 量
chú   lù   piàn   nèi   kē   gǎn   liáng

Exercise: Describe the following pictures.

1. 看病

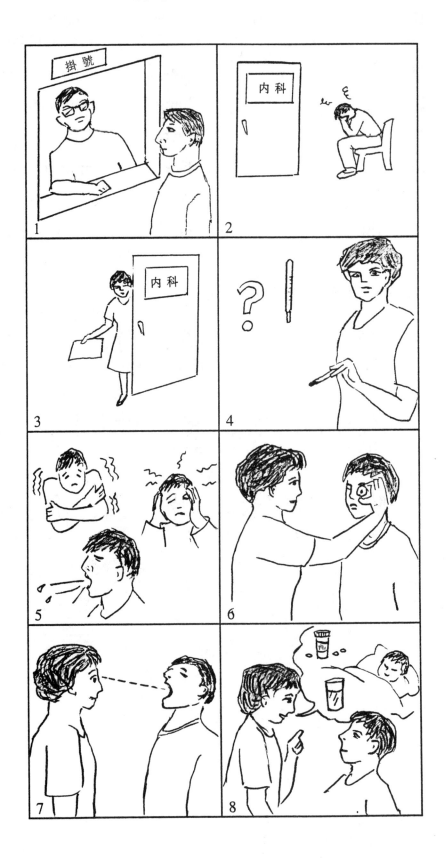

2. 借書

LESSONS 48 & 49

GRAMMAR NOTES

l. Notional Passive Sentence

- 藥已經吃完了 。

- 作業交給老師了沒有 ？

- 飯已經作好了 ， 菜還沒開始作呢 。

- 這個照像機還能修好嗎?

- 屋子打掃乾淨了。

Sentences like the above are very common in everyday conversation. They are passive in meaning, because the subjects are the recipients instead of the doers of the actions. The doers are not mentioned because there is no need to name them or they are already implied from the context.

2. Passive Sentences with Prepositions 被 /讓 /叫

In these passive sentences the passive meaning is more emphasized and the doers can be indicated. The sentence patterns are:

Recipient	Adverbial / Optative Verb	Preposition 被 /讓 /叫	Doer	Verb	Other element(s)
1. 王老師		被	學生	請	去參加生日晚會了。
2. 照像機		讓	人	借	走了。
3. 作業		叫	狗	吃	了。
4. 我的信	不能	讓	你	看。	
5. 車	會不會	被		偷？	
6. 那本書	沒有	被		翻譯	成法文。
7. 自行車	常常	被		騎	壞。

Notes:

1) The three prepositions 被／讓／叫 have the same meaning, but 被 is more formal than 讓 and 叫, and can be used both in written and spoken forms while 讓 and 叫 are usually used in speech.

2) The predicate verb usually cannot stand by itself. It is either followed by "other element(s)," such as an aspect particle (過／着／了), an object or a complement to indicate the result, degree or time of the action; or it is preceded by an adverbial or an optative verb.

3) When there is no need to name the doers, or when it is difficult to name the doers, 人 can be used as a general reference as in sentence 2.

4) Sometimes the doer is not mentioned at all. In this case the preposition 被 should be used instead of 讓／叫 , and the verb follows immediately after 被 as in sentences 5, 6 & 7.

5) Negative adverbs should be before the prepositions as in sentences 4 & 6.

xx 那本書被沒有翻譯成法文。 xx

3. Interrogative Pronouns Expressing General Denotation

Interrogative pronouns followed by 都 or 也 can be used in declarative sentences to express general denotation:

甚麼	any, every
誰	whoever, everybody
哪兒 ／甚麼地方	wherever, everywhere
甚麼時候	whenever, anytime
怎麼(+ verb)	in whatever way, no matter how

帕蘭卡病了， 今天甚麼都沒吃， 甚麼地方也沒去。
她躺在床上休息， 誰打的電話她都不接。古波讓她去
醫院， 可是怎麼說她也不去。

老師： 要是你有問題 ， 甚麼時候都可以來問。
學生： 我問過了， 可是你怎麼講我都不懂。

49

A: 車應該停在哪兒？

B: 哪兒都可以停。

　　小謝不買書，可是甚麼書都想看，哪個朋友的書
他都借。他的同學小張書架上的哪本小説他都看過。

　　Adverb 也 is more often used in negative sentences, while 都 can be used in both positive and negative sentences.

4. Summary of Measure Words

動量詞　　<u>Verb Measure Words</u>

遍　　　　再看一遍

次　　　　去了兩次

名量詞　　<u>Noun Measure Words</u>

班	這班學生	刻	三刻 (鐘)
杯	一杯桔子水 /牛奶/酒	塊	幾塊 (錢)?
本	那本書/雜誌/本子	輛	那輛公共汽車 /自行車
層	幾層 (樓)?	毛	五毛(錢)
寸	三寸, 五英寸	米	三米(高)
尺	一尺 , 三英尺	片	兩片藥/面包
點	幾點(鐘)?	瓶	一瓶酒 /桔子水
度	零下三度	束	一束花
分	五分(鐘)	雙	一雙手 /筷子/鞋
幅	那幅畫兒	歲	幾歲了 ?
個	每個人 /桔子 /球	套	一套書 /郵票 /衣服
公斤	五公斤半	條	那條河/裙子/褲子/魚/路
壺	一壺酒 /茶/水	碗	一碗飯 /粥/湯
間	那間教室/屋子	位	一位老師 /作家 /客人

家	一家咖啡館 /飯館 /書店	些	一些學生 /人 /火腿 /問題
架	一架飛機 /照像機	元	五萬元 (錢)
角	三角 (錢)	座	那座山 /牆 /橋
斤	幾斤？	張	每張桌子 /票 /報
句	一句句子 /話	隻	一隻箱子 /眼睛
課	一課課文，第一課 (書)	種	這種習慣 /東西

SUPPLEMENTARY TEXT　　　　補 充 課 文

　　帕蘭卡好了，古波 把她從醫院接回來了。

　　帕蘭卡立刻給媽媽打了一個電話 ，讓她放心。媽媽説：我和你爸爸下個月要來中國看你 ，你希望我們甚麽時候來？帕蘭卡高興地説："太好了！ 你們下個月哪天來都可以 。我們快要放暑假了，我和古波每天都有空兒。"

　　帕蘭卡去古波的宿舍告訴他這個消息的時候， 他正在看劇本《茶館》呢。他指着書説: " 我請你爸爸媽媽看話劇 《茶館》吧。這個話劇不但寫得好 ，而且演得也很成功 。誰都説應該看。這是有名的作家老舍寫的 ，已經翻譯成英文和法文了。 現在票還沒賣完，我今天就去買 ，下個月就買不到了 。"

　　帕蘭卡覺得古波的屋子太亂了— 地圖和報在地上放 着；茶杯沒有洗 ，箱子開着 ； 鞋在書架上擺着；自行車放在床前邊 。她説: "爸爸媽媽來了以後 ，一定會來你宿舍看看。你的屋子比誰的都亂......" 古波不好意思地説: "箱子裡的東西太多了，怎麼關也關不上 。自行車讓我同屋騎壞了 ，

還沒修好呢。地圖叫風從牆上刮下來了……" 帕蘭卡問: "鞋是不是也被刮到書架上了？" 古波笑著説: "好了，好了，我知道你的屋子比我的整齊。你爸爸媽媽來的時候，我一定把屋子打掃乾淨; 可是今天我打掃不了－我的吸塵器壞了。"

NEW WORDS　　生　詞

1.	被	prep.	bèi	(prepositon used in passive sentences)
2.	讓	prep.	ràng	(preposition used in passive sentences)
3.	叫	prep.	jiào	(preposition used in passive sentences)
4.	消息	n	xiāoxi	news, information
5.	茶館	n	cháguǎn	teahouse
6.	演	v	yǎn	to perform, to act
7.	成功	adj	chénggōng	successful
8.	屋子	n	wūzi	room
9.	亂	adj	luàn	disordered, untidy, messy
10.	打掃	v	dǎsǎo	to clean up
11.	乾净	adj	gānjing	clean, neat and tidy
12.	劇本	n	jùběn	play script
13.	書架	n	shūjià	bookshelf
14.	吸塵器	n	xīchénqì	vacuum cleaner

LEARN CHARACTERS

被、　演、　屋、　亂(乱)、　乾(干)、　净
bèi　　yǎn　　wū　　luàn　　　　gān　　　　jìng

┌───┐
│ **MAJOR GRAMMAR POINTS COVERED**   │
│   │
│ **IN ELEMANTARY CHINESE**   │
└───┘

1.　Parts of Speech

Noun

general	太陽, 母親, 醫院
location	中間, 東, 上 , 外邊
time	年, 月, 小時, 最近, 一會兒
proper	北京, 天安門

Pronoun

personal	她, 我們, 自己, 大家
interrogative	誰, 哪 , 怎麼樣, 甚麼
demonstrative	這兒, 那, 這些
other	每, 別的 , 有的, 這麼

Verb

reduplication (<u>AB</u><u>AB</u>)	休息休息, 玩兒玩兒, 等一等
optative	要, 願意 , 應該
functions as subject	學習開始了.
functions as attributive	吃的東西 , 工作的時間
functions as object	喜歡游泳
functions as complement	看得懂, 作完 , 過來
functions as adverbial	注意地聽, 關心地問

Adjective

reduplication (<u>AA</u><u>BB</u>)	舒舒服服 , 高高興興
functions as attributive	舊雜誌

53

functions as predicate	他很着急
functions as adverbial	多花了十塊錢，認真地介紹
functions as complement	準備好, 説不清楚
functions as subject	貴沒關係

Numeral

| cardinal | 零, 十, 百, 千, 萬 , 億 |
| ordinal | 第三 |

Measure

| for noun | 件, 輛, 座, 幅, 種, 些, 雙, 束, 歲, 套 , 尺 |
| for verb | 次, 遍 , 回 |

Adverb

negative	不, 沒有, 別 , 不要
time	才, 就 , 常常 , 正在, 總是, 剛
	已經, 永遠
degree	很, 太, 更, 非常, 真, 多麼
repetition	又, 還, 再 , 也
scope	都, 一共 , 衹, 一起
inquiry	多

Preposition   在, 從, 往, 跟, 對, 為, 比, 給, 把, 除了

Conjunction   和 , 跟, 要是, 只有, 還是 , 或者

雖然 ......但是 /可是......

因為 ......所以 ......

不但 ......而且 ......

Particle

structural	的, 地, 得
aspectual	了, 着, 過
modal	嗎, 呢 , 吧, 啊, 了

2. Aspects of Action
1. Completion (with 了)　　　　我寄了一封信 。

　　　　　　　　　　　　　我吃了晚飯就睡覺了 。

2. Change/new situation (with 了)　天氣熱了。

3. Imminent future (with 要...了)　考試要開始了。

4. In progress (with 正/正在/在...呢 or .... 呢)

　　　　　　　　　　　　你進來的時候, 我正打電話呢。

　　　　　　　　　　　　他沒有看電視, 他睡覺呢 。

5. Continuation (with 着)　　　他穿着一雙新鞋 。

6. Past experience (with 過)　　我沒有住過醫院 。 你住過嗎 ？

3. Questions
1. with 嗎　　　　　　　　你頭疼嗎 ？

2. with 好/對/可以 + 嗎　　我用一下你的詞典 ，好嗎?

3. with 吧　　　　　　　　我們應該往右拐吧 ？

4. with interrogative pronouns 洛杉磯的天氣怎麼樣? 冬天多少度 ？

5. with 多　　　　　　　　你有多高 ？

6. with 呢　　　　　　　　你的票呢 ？

　　　　　　　　　　　　我又累又餓 , 你呢 ？

7. with 還是　　　　　　　豆腐好吃還是火腿好吃 ？

8. with "affirmative verb + negative verb"

　　　　　　　　　　　　你聽得見聽不見? 你聽見了沒有 ？

9. with 是不是　　　　　　長城是不是在中國 ？

4. Comparison
1. with 比/不比　　　　　　雖然他只比我高一點兒 (他比我高半英寸)。 可是他跑得比我快得多 。

2. with 跟......一樣　　　　他的車跟我的車一樣新 。

3. with 有/沒有　　　　　美國人沒有中國人多。

4. with 更 and 最　　　　中文難, 日文更難。 哪國文最難 ？

5.　　Complements

1. Result　　　　　　　寫完, 整理好, 打開

2. Direction
   　simple　　　　　　Verb + 來/去

   　compound　　　　　Verb + 上 /下 /進 /出 /回/過/起 + 來/去

3. Degree　　　　　　　游得很快, 高興得跳起來

4. Potential　　　　　　搬得動, 站不起來

5. Time-measure　　　　住三年, 等十分鐘, 看一會兒

6. Action-measure　　　看一遍 , 去三次

7. Quantity　　　　　　他比我大三歲。

6.　　Types of Sentences

1. Declarative　　　　　她是醫生。

2. Interrogative　　　　內科病房在哪兒 ？

3. Imperative　　　　　站住, 別動！

4. Exclamatory　　　　這個故事太沒有意思了！

　　　　　　　　　　　今天的天氣太好了!

7.　　Predicates of Sentence

1. Verbal　　　　　　　我不告訴你。

2. Adjectival　　　　　那個孩子很聰明。

3. Nominal　　　　　　今天星期四 。

4. Subject-predicate　　他身體不好, 總是頭疼。

8.　　Special Patterns of Sentences with Verbal Predicates

1. Two objects　　　　　王老師教我們語法。

2. Verb/verb phrase as object　　我不喜歡聽古典音樂 。

3. Subject-predicate construction as object

你覺得中文難嗎？

4. Preposed object　　　　　　　你買的那套書我也買了 。

5. Verbal construction in series我每天騎自行車去學校上課 。

6. Pivotal　　　　　　　　　　他請我去他家玩兒。

7. 是 ……的 structure for emphasis

你是幾點來的？跟誰一起來的？

8. 把 structure　　　　　　　　你把我的錄音機放在哪兒了 ？

9. 被 structure　　　　　　　　窗戶被 (讓/叫)人打破了。

10. Existential　　　　　　　　後邊有一個醫院。

內科病房不在左邊 。

茶杯旁邊是藥 。

9.　　Complex　Sentences

1. Coordinate　　　　　　有的坐公共汽車去 ，有的騎自行車去 。

他又會踢足球，又喜歡畫畫兒。

2. Condition　　　　　　要是你喜歡這個照像機，我就送你 。

他一看見我 ，就高興地走過來。

只有不吸煙不喝酒,身體才會健康 。

只要努力，就一定學得好 。

3. Cause & Result　　　　他因為病得很厲害,所以沒來上課 。

4. Adversative　　　　　這種魚雖然很貴 ，但是買的人很多 。

5. Progressive　　　　　這位美國人不但會説法語,

而且會説日語和漢語。

6. Inclusion & Exclusion

我們班除了小張以外,別人都不會日文。

除了這件游泳衣以外, 我還買了一件襯衫 。

PART II

HOMEWORK

HOMEWORK (Lesson 36)

Name _____

Section _____

T. A. _____

I. Write out the following figures in characters.

1.   321   2.   7,890

3.   65,042   4.   976,804

5.   123,000,000

II. Write out the following prices in characters.

1.   ¥0.25   2.   ¥21.50

3.   ¥105.10   4.   ¥4,367.99

III. Translate the following dialog into Chinese.

A: How much is the movie at 7:00 in the evening?

B: Seven dollars. How many do you want?

A: Four.

B: Twenty eight dollars (all together).

A: Here is thirty.

B: Two dollars is your change.

IV. Answer the following questions in Chinese according to the information given. Write in complete sentences.

	北京	洛杉磯
冬天	長/很冷	短/不冷
自行車	四百萬	三十萬
外國留學生	一萬多	兩萬五
中國餐館	兩千多個	六百多個
飛機場	大	更大

61

1.   Is the winter in Los Angeles as long as the winter in Beijing?

2.   Are there more people riding bicycles in Beijing than in L.A.?

3.   Are there as many foreign students in Beijing as in L.A.?

4.   Are there more Chinese restaurants in L.A. than in Beijing?

5.   Is Beijing Airport bigger than L.A. Airport?

V. Write five complete sentences, comparing 古波 and 小張 in the following aspects.

	古波	小張
看電影	每個月五次	每個月一次
起床	8:30	7:30
開車	每小時 70英里	每小時 45 英里
學習	每天 4 小時	每天 8 小時
打籃球	更好	好

1.

2.

3.

4.

5.

HOMEWORK (Lesson 37)

Name _____

Section _____

T. A. _____

I. Rewrite the following sentences to show the exact difference as shown in the example.

他今年四十歲，他太太今年三十六歲 。 -> 他比他太太大四歲。

(or: 他太太比他小四歲 。)

1. 我的灰襯衫是八號的 ， 我的藍襯衫是十號的 。（大／小）

2. 王老師早上八點到學校 ，謝老師早上十點到學校 。（早v／晚v）

3. 我同屋上星期工作了八小時 ， 他這星期工作了十小時 。
   （多v／少v）

4. 王大夫的新自行車一千九百五十塊 ，他兒子的舊汽車一千五
   百五十塊。（貴／便宜）

5. 昨天洛杉磯九十度 ，北京也九十度。（冷／熱）

II. Fill in the blanks with 不但 ...而且 ..../因為...所以 .../雖然 ...但是 .../要是...就....

1. 這條褲子_____ 太短了, _____ 也太肥了。

2. _____ 他吃得很多, _____ 他瘦極了 。

3. 他 _____ 打球打得很好, _____ 騎馬 (mǎ, horse) 也騎得很好。

4. _____ 你以後想去日本工作 ，你現在 _____ 應該開始學日文。

III. Answer the following questions in Chinese according to the information provided. Write in complete sentences.

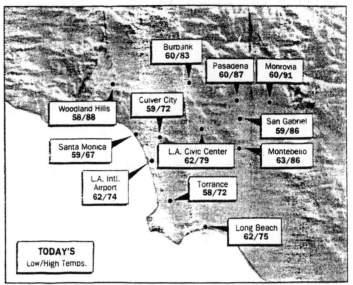

1.   Which city is the hottest during the day (白天 báitiān)? Which cities are the coolest at night?

2.   At night, how much cooler is Pasadena than Long Beach?

3.   During the day, how much hotter is San Gabriel than Santa Monica?

4.   Is L.A. International Airport as hot as the L.A. Civic Center (市中心, shì zhōngxīn) during the day?

5.   How is the weather (both during the day and at night) of Woodland Hills compared to the weather of Culver City?

IV. Write a composition of 8 sentences, comparing yourself and a friend of yours.

HOMEWORK (Lesson 38)

Name _____

Section _____

T. A. _____

I. Translate the following sentences into Chinese.

1. A: Did you see Xiao Zhang in the classroom today?
    B: No, I didn't, but I saw his roommate.

2. Prof. Wang didn't say clearly whether he wanted us to turn in our composition tomorrow or the day after tomorrow. I just called him, but I dialed thewrong number.

3. I'm afraid (think) we took the wrong bus. Bus #7 should turn right on Garden Blvd., not on College Blvd.

4. My sister broke my bicycle (while riding it). I haven't finished fixing it yet.

5. The plane flying to Beijing is going to take off soon. Please get on board.

II. Make a sentence with each of the following structures.

1. 又...... 又......

2. 不但...... 而且......

3. 要是...... 就......

III. Give directions according to the map given.

1. 你朋友從宿舍給你打電話，想來你家玩兒， 請你告訴他怎麼走。

2. 你在圖書館看完了書，要去銀行工作，你怎麼走？

3. 你和你的朋友看完電影以後想去餐館吃飯 ， 你們應該怎麼走？

4. 有一個人在公園裏病了，他的朋友要送他去醫院。 他們應該怎麼走？

5. 你在飛機場接了朋友以後要和他一起去王老師家,你應該怎麼走？

6. 喝了咖啡以後你要去郵局寄掛號信 ，你怎麼走？

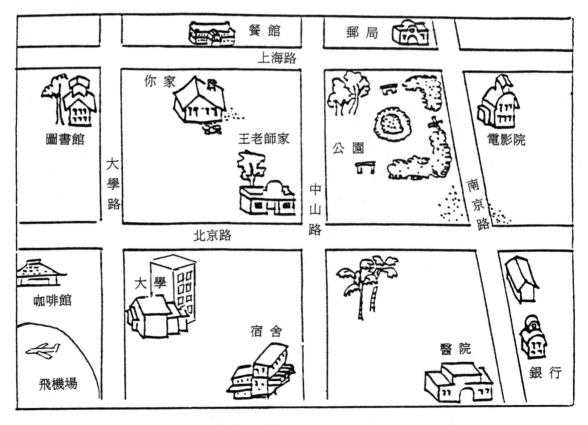

HOMEWORK (Lesson 39)

Name _____

Section _____

T. A. _____

I. Fill in the blanks:

A. with 到, 在, 開, 住

1) 我不要坐_____前邊 , 我想坐_____後邊。

2) 張阿姨收 _____她女兒的信以後 , 一定要離開洛杉磯回 _____她女兒那兒。 我們沒有留_____她 。

3) 我打_____箱子以後 , 看見我放_____裏邊的茶壺和茶杯都破 (pò, broken) 了。

4) 我的名字我已經告訴過他十幾次了 , 可是他還沒有記 _____。

5) 我叔叔的地址我寫 _____本子上了, 可是我沒找_____我的本子。

B. with了, 吧 , 呢

1) – 你下星期能看完這本書 _____?
    – 我能看完, 你 _____?

2) – 我們聽甚麼_____?
    – 我們聽新聞廣播_____。

3) – 聽 , 刮風_____。
    – 還下 着雨_____。

4) – 他們在看病 _____?
    – 不, 他們檢查身體 _____。

5) – 我太忙 _____, 今天不想去看電影 _____。
    – 沒關係, 我們明天去 _____。

II. Reduplicate the following adjectives and then put them in the appropriate blanks:

客氣 ， 認真 ， 漂亮 ， 清楚 ， 高興

1. 她 ＿＿＿＿＿＿ 地跟他説: " 對不起，我今天沒空兒。 "

2. 她今天穿着一條 ＿＿＿＿＿＿ 的裙子; ＿＿＿＿＿＿ 地來參加舞會。

3. 他每天都 ＿＿＿＿＿＿ 地練習寫漢字。

4. 雖然那是十年以前的事 ，我現在還記得 ＿＿＿＿＿＿。

III. Translate the following sentences into Chinese.

As soon as we finished eating dinner, my aunt and uncle wanted to leave. My dad asked them to stay to listen to my younger brother singing. He sang a Chinese song for them. They said he is a smart kid.

IV. Composition: Write a letter to your friend, telling him/her about your life at school. Use resultative complements when possible.

HOMEWORK (Lesson 41/43)

Name _____

Section _____

T. A. _____

I. Translate the following sentences into Chinese.

1.   A: Did you bring your camera with you? Please come over and take a picture for us.

        B: I'm sorry, I don't have time now. I have to go to class. I am already late.

2.   Because my brother did not write to me from China, I mailed a letter to his school again. (use directional complement)

3.   (A and B are both inside the movie theater)

        A: Look, the person who just walked in is Professor Zhang.

        B: Let's go over there to talk to him.

4.   A: Is that Chinese dictionary yours ?

        B: It's another student's. Mine I've already taken home.

5.   A: Would you like to swim across the river?

        B: No. I'm both thirsty and hungry now.

        A: I'm a little tired, too. Let's go back to the dorm.

II. Make a sentence with each of the following phrases.

1.　　寄回來

2.　　穿過去

3.　　拿下來

4.　　跑出去

5.　　開進來

6.　　站起來

III. Describe the following pictures. (At least 2 sentences for each picture.)

1.

2.

3.

HOMEWORK (Lesson 42)

Name _____

Section _____

T. A. _____

I. Translate the following sentences into Chinese. Use potential complement structure when appropriate.

1. (In a post office. A is a customer. B is a postman.)
    A: Will he be able to receive this letter tomorrow?
    B: I cannot understand (by reading) the address that you wrote. If you
        write clearly, I think he will (then) be able to receive it tomorrow.

2. A: How many people can this cinema accommodate (by sitting)?
    B: It can accommodate about 1,200 people.
    A: It is extremely big! When my friend comes in, do you think he can find us?
    B: I don't think he can find us. Let's wait for him at the entrance (door).

3. A: Can you move a desk this heavy by yourself?
    B: Yes, I can. I am not afraid of doing heavy work.

II. Fill in the blanks with proper potential complements:

1. 中文小説你看 _____ 嗎?

2. 這輛自行車太舊了, 你修 _____修 _____?

3. 你的房間很小, 住 _____ 五個人嗎?

4. 這個行李太重了, 你拿 _____ 嗎?

71

5. 買一張電影票用 _____ 十塊錢嗎？

6. 今天的練習不多，我一小時就能作 _____ 。

7. 那座山太高，我爬_____。

8. 你一天記 _____ 多少生詞？

9. 這條河這麼大，你游 _____ 游_____？

10. 老師病了，明天上 _____課。

II. Change the following statements into questions, using 是不是 .

1. 他孫子每天晚上都不停地哭。

2. 他們怕幹重活兒。

3. 在海邊的大石頭上坐 着的那個人正在唱歌。

4. 在洛杉磯坐公共汽車很不方便 。

I. 是…的 Construction

Make questions for the following sentences focusing on the underlined parts, and then answer the questions, e.g.,

我昨天中午在學校吃了午飯。

Q:　你昨天中午是在哪兒吃的午飯？

A:　我昨天中午是在學校吃的午飯。

1.　我同屋去年在北京外語學院學習中文。

Q:　_____

A:　_____

2.　他昨天跟美國代表團一起坐飛機到了北京。

Q:　_____

A:　_____

3.　我一九九五年來加州大學學習中國文學。

Q:　_____

A:　_____

4.　小張跟他爸爸媽媽去上海旅行了。

Q:　_____

A:　_____

5.　　小張從北京大學畢業了。

Q: _____

A: _____

II. Translate the following sentences into Chinese.

1.　　A:　　What beautiful scenery! Look at the boats and the bridge on the lake!
　　　B:　　It is really like a painting.

2.　　(Use 是…的 structure. The underlined phrases indicate the focus.)
　　　A:　　I heard that you have traveled to Beijing. <u>When</u> did you go?
　　　B:　　I went to Beijing <u>last summer</u>.
　　　A:　　Did you go <u>by yourself</u>?
　　　B:　　I went there <u>with my schoolmates.</u> We didn't go <u>for fun</u>. We went to <u>study international trade.</u>

III. 複習漢字： Write characters with the following radicals:

氵： _____, _____, _____, _____, _____

扌： _____, _____, _____, _____, _____

灬： _____, _____, _____, _____, _____

辶： _____, _____, _____, _____, _____

HOMEWORK (Lesson 46/47)

Name _____

Section _____

T. A. _____

I. Make sentences with the following phrases:

     e.g., 掛/畫/在牆上

        我把畫掛在牆上了。

1.   送/病人/到病房去

2.   沒有寫/那個字/清楚

3.   放/錄音機/在桌子上

4.   吃/感冒藥/完了

5.   搬/行李/到車上去

6.   忘/本子/在教室裏

II. Change the following sentences into sentences with 把-structure:

     e.g., 他開走了我的船。---> 他把我的船開走了。

1.   他花完了他母親的錢。

2.   這位大夫能看好你妻子的病。

3.   工人們下個月就能修好湖上的那座大橋。

4.   我一打開電視，爺爺就關上了他的收音機。

III. Translation:

1.   A: How do you feel today? Do you feel a little better?
          B: I do not cough as badly as yesterday, but I still have a fever and
              a headache. The doctor told me to take this medicine four times
              a day, two pills each time.

2.   Except for Zhisou, all the others think that Yugong is smart.

3.   In addition to climbing mountains, I also like to travel and play football.

IV. 複習漢字   Write out the characters you know with the following radicals:

木 ：

糸 ：

金 ：

言 ：

食 ：

HOMEWORK (Lesson 48/49)

Name _____

Section _____

T. A. _____

I. Change the following sentences into passive sentences with 被 / 叫/ 讓 .
Make other changes when necessary.

　　　e.g., 小張把我的車借走了。 --> 我的車被（or 叫/讓）小張借走了.

1.　　我的狗把我的作業 (zuòyè, homework) 吃了。

2.　　我同屋用壞了我的新照像機。

3.　　有人把 Shakespeare 的書都翻譯成中文了。

4.　　風把我給我女朋友寫的詩都刮走了。

5.　　我弟弟把我的茶杯都打破了。

6.　　我爸爸已經把自行車修好了。

7.　　他把屋子打掃得很乾淨。

8.　　我把信封上的地址寫錯了。

II.　　Fill in the blanks with the following interrogative pronouns:
　　　　　誰, 甚麼, 哪兒 , 怎麼, 甚麼時候

1.　　那個箱子很重, 我 _____ 搬都搬不動。

2. 我今天早上 _____ 都沒吃，所以現在餓極了。

3. 我們班除了我以外，_____ 也不想去中國工作。

4. 他今天不舒服，_____ 都不想去。

5. 我的眼鏡 (yǎnjìng, glasses) 我 _____ 找也找不到，現在我 _____ 都看不清楚。

6. 她真漂亮，穿 _____ 衣服都好看。

7. 王老師很熱情，學生 _____ 去問他問題，他都很歡迎。

8. 我覺得漢字太難了，_____ 寫也寫不好看。

III. Translate the following sentences into Chinese:

1. A: How was the play that you saw last night?
   B: It was excellent. The play was not only well written, but also well performed. Everybody liked it. The tickets for next month are already sold out.

2. A: How should we answer this question?
   B: You may answer in whatever way you want.

APPENDIX A

Key to the Exercises in Lessons 36-50　　練習答案

第三十六課

2.　(1) 這種筆比那種（筆）便宜。
　　(2) 他的歷史知識比我（的歷史知識）多。
　　(3) 這學期他比我進步得快。（這學期他進步得比我快。）
　　(4) 我每天比他睡得早。
　　(5) 他比他朋友大。
　　(6) 古波看中國電影比帕蘭卡看得多。
　　(7) 今天比昨天（更）熱。
　　(8) 他妹妹比他（更）會開車。

3.　(1) 那種自行車的質量沒有這種（自行車）好。
　　(2) 我去年沒有今年忙。
　　(3) 我們學校的郵局沒有這個郵局大。
　　(4) 我的成績沒有他好。
　　(5) 這個男同志寫字寫得沒有那個女同志好看。
　　(6) 我的身體沒有我同學健康。

第三十七課

2.　(1) 他的工作跟他愛人一樣　　　。
　　(2) 我以後學的專業跟我朋友 (學的) 一樣。
　　(3) 古波買的詞典跟帕蘭卡(買的)一樣。
　　(4) 小王跟小張一樣大。
　　(5) 他學法語的時間跟你一樣長。
　　(6) 我跟我弟弟一樣高。

3.　(1) 老工廠多多少工人，老工廠多
　　(2) 這件長多少，這件長
　　(3) 他妹妹大幾歲，他妹妹大
　　(4) 這輛車便宜多少錢，這輛便宜

(5) 他同學早到學校幾分鐘，他同學早到
(6) 他們班少學了多少課，他們班少學了

5. (1) 這種布多少錢一米？
   (2) 你的鞋比我的小一點兒，我穿不太合適。
   (3) 這個店定作的衣服比那個店好看得多。
   (4) 這個月比上月冷一些。
   (5) 今天很晚了，下次我再來吧。
   (6) 明天你能騎車來嗎？要不，我開車去接你？

第三十八課

2. 聽　聽見
   (1) 聽，聽見，聽見
   (2) 聽，聽見，聽見
   (3) 聽，聽，聽

   看 看見
   (1) 看，看見，看見
   (2) 看見
   (3) 看，看見，看，看見

3. (1) 懂　(2) 對　(3) 到（懂）　(4) 錯　(5) 好　(6) 會

5. (1) 老師，"帶"字怎麼寫？
   (2) 他剛起床，還沒有吃早飯呢。
   (3) 你知道這是甚麼方向嗎？這是南邊。
   (4) 這個詞中文怎麼說？
   (5) 他講語法講得怎麼樣？
   (6) 這件衣服太肥，請您給我換一件，好嗎？
   (7) 你跑得比我快得多。

第三十九課

2. (1) 鍛煉完，鍛煉完
   (2) 談完，談完
   (3) 找到（照片），找到
   (4) 接到（你叔叔），沒有接到
   (5) 記住，我還沒有記住

3. (1) 他找了一上午，還沒有找到那個地方。
   (2) 星期六晚上，他們跳完舞已經快十二點了。

(3) 今年暑假他要留在北京。

(4) 李老師對同學們非常關心。

(5) 請大家明天交練習本子。

(6) 這句話是甚麼意思？

(7) 這位售票員對大家非常熱情。

(8) 雖然在她家的時間不長，但是他們過得很愉快。

(9) 這個意思中文怎麼說？

(10) 丁雲一收到帕蘭卡的信就給她回了一封信。

第四十課

1.　上飛機，上火車，上汽車，上電車，上樓，上課
　　下飛機，下火車，下汽車，下電車，下樓，下課，
　　下雨，下雪
　　開門，開車，開花，開學
　　打電話，打球，打太極拳
　　接電話，接球，接信，接人
　　看書，看報，看電影，看電視，看京劇，看朋友，看病
　　服務員，營業員，售票員，運動員
　　孩子，桔子，裙子，房子，桌子，椅子，筷子，箱子，
　　鼻子，葉子，牌子，綢子，本子，旗子

2.　(1) 這個車間比那個車間大。

　　(2) 語言學院的學生比鋼鐵學院的學生少得多。

　　(3) 帕蘭卡騎自行車沒有古波騎得快。

　　(4) 這套衣服比那套便宜十二塊錢，這套的質量沒有那套好。

　　(5) 這個工廠的生產發展得有沒有那個工廠快？

　　(6) 這輛汽車的顏色跟那輛一樣。

　　(7) 你聽的故事跟我講的一樣不一樣？

　　(8) 他學過的生詞跟你一樣多，可是他記住的生詞沒有你多。

　　(9) 我們班上小王打太極拳打得最好。

　　(10) 我更喜歡看京劇。

3.　(1) 嗎，了　　　(2) 了，吧
　　(3) 嗎，呢　　　(4) 呢，吧　　　(5) 了，呢

4.　（打）完，（收）到，（收）到，（上）完，（騎）到，
　　（看）見，（站）在，（坐）在，（跑）到

6.　(1) 新馬路比舊馬路長。

　　(2) 這個公園比那個公園大一點兒。

81

(3) 今天晚上我作完了練習就看電視。

(4) 這套茶具跟那套一樣。

(5) 他聽見有人敲門 。

(6) 今天比昨天冷 。

(7) 我看見他在那兒。

(8) 他這次考試成績不比她高。

(9) 哥哥比妹妹大三歲 。

(10) 她爸爸希望他們學好中文。

第四十一課

2.　(1) 去　　　(2) 去　　　(3) 來　　　(4) 去　　　(5) 來
3.　(1) 就下來 （就來）　　(2) 就過來歡迎他們

　　(3) 就穿了一件薄衣服　(4) 就去買了三本回來

　　(5) 就不會坐錯了車了　(6) 就不定作棉襖了
4.　(1) 對不起 ， 我忘了這件事兒了。

　　(2) 對不起 ， 我想打個電話， 可以嗎?

　　(3) 運動會九點才開始呢? 他八點就到操場來了 。

　　(4) 這個建築我早就聽說了， 今天才有機會來參觀 。

　　(5) 小張不在家， 他剛出去， 一會兒就回來。

　　(6) 我不進去了， 請你告訴他: 明天我們到故宮去 。

　　(7) 上月哥哥給我買來了兩本中國小說 ， 我給妹妹送去了一本。

　　(8) 要是公共汽車太擠 ， 我們就騎自行車去 。
5.　(1) 早早　　　(2) 客客氣氣　　　(3) 清清楚楚

　　(4) 漂漂亮亮　　(5) 認認真真

第四十二課

2.　(1) 得見 ， 不見　(2) 得動 ， 得動　(3) 得下， 得下

　　(4) 得了， 不了　(5) 得到， 不到　(6) 得到， 得到

　　(7) 得了， 得了　(8) 得去， 不去
3.　(1) 老師用中文講語法 ， 你聽得懂聽不懂?

　　　 他講得很慢， 也很清楚， 我聽得懂 。

　　(2) 學校的禮堂坐得下坐不下兩千人 ?

　　　 這個禮堂很大， 坐得下兩千人 。

　　(3) 今天上午見得到見不到那位顧問 ?

　　　 上午他去檢查工作了 ， 見不到他。

(4) 你們學院修建的新樓今年完得成完不成？
　　工人們都在努力幹，今年完得成。
(5) 我們不坐車了，你走得動走不動？
　　路不太遠，我走得動。
(6) 這個照像機的鏡頭修得好修不好？
　　這個照像機的鏡頭修得好。
(7) 這首古詩的意思你看得懂看不懂？
　　這首古詩生詞很多，我看不懂。
(8) 他們的問題你現在回答得了回答不了？
　　我要想一想，我現在回答不了。

5.　七千五百六十二　　　八千零五十
　　一千一　（百）　　　一萬

6.　(1) 這座城已經有三千多年的歷史了。
　　(2) 這條馬路有多寬？聽説最寬的地方有一百米。
　　(3) 那個工人還沒有來，現在禮堂的門開不開。
　　(4) 這是典型的中國古典音樂。
　　(5) 你這麼喜歡藝術，為甚麼學習語言專業呢？
　　(6) 他今天這麼忙，我以後再去找他吧。

第四十三課

2.　(1) 過來，過去　(2) 進去　　(3) 下來，過來
　　(4) 起來　　　　(5) 下來　　(6) 上來（過來）
　　(7) 回去　　　　(8) 出來　　(9) 回，去
3.　(1) 上來　　　　(2) 出去　　(3) 回來　(4) 下來　　(5) 進，去
　　(6) 上，去，下來　　(7) 出，來　　(8) 回，去
5.　(1) 他今天幹了一天的活兒，現在有點餓了。
　　(2) 今天比較冷，你的衣服夠不夠？
　　(3) 這兒還有別的飯館嗎？
　　(4) 他又會照像，又會洗照片。
　　(5) 本市今年修建了好幾條新馬路。
　　(6) 上海風味的菜不是很好吃嗎？
　　(7) 他對各種顧客都服務得很周到。

第四十四課

2.　(1) 她是昨天晚上去廣州的。

(2) 他是坐公共汽車去的天安門 。

(3) 她是跟她母親一起去頤和園的 。

(4) 不，他是從日本坐船來的 。

(5) 不，他是到中國來旅行的 。

(6) 他是為幫助建設工廠來南京的。（他是來幫助建設工廠的。 ）

4. (1) 他是甚麼時候決定來中國旅行的 ？

(2) 時間過得多麼快啊！

(3) 只有學好古漢語，才能研究中國的古詩。

(4) 我們多麼希望明天能出太陽啊！

(5) 看球賽的時候，觀眾激動得大聲地喊 。

(6) 春天來了，公園裡的樹一天比一天綠了。

第四十五課

1. 花園，公園，動物園，頤和園，園林

圖書館，咖啡館，大使館，飯館，博物館

閱覽室，臥室

操場，廣場，機場

食堂，禮堂，人民大會堂

客廳，餐廳

廚房，書房，房子，房間

4. (1) 就，才　　(2) 才　　(3) 才　　(4) 就　　(5) 就　　(6) 才

5. (1) 他們的孩子非常可愛 。

(2) 他想去動物園，又想去頤和園，到現在還決定不了 。

(3) 我是三年前離開農村的，後來就到這個工廠工作了 。

(4) 他希望學會畫畫兒，又不願意花時間練習 ，所以總是學不好 。

(6) 這張珍貴的照片是二十年以前照的 。

6. (1) +　　(2) −　　(3) +　　(4) −　　(5) −

(6) −　　(7) +　　(8) −　　(9) −　　(10) +

第四十六課

2. (1) 我把窗戶開開了。

(2) 我已經把這本小說看完了。

(3) 她把你的錄音機帶來了 。

(4) 小蘭已經把葡萄洗好了。

(5) 他已經把這本雜誌送給我了 。

(6) 他已經把這件事兒告訴我了。

3. (1) 他把這封航空信寄走了 。
   (2) 他把這些東西包好了。
   (3) 他把上一課的生詞記住了。
   (4) 他把一百米的記錄打破了。
   (5) 他把那個故事講完了 。
   (6) 他把他朋友送回家了。

4. (1) 他們今年能把這座樓修建好嗎？
   (2) 我可以把這本小説帶回去嗎？
   (3) 你放心，我不會把這件事兒忘了。
   (4) 他不知道大夫能不能把他的病看好。
   (5) 小蘭幫助姥姥把客人留住了 。
   (6) 天冷了，你應該把棉襖穿上了 。
   (7) 他在花園裡種了很多花兒，又種了一些樹 。
   (8) 我今天頭疼，又有點兒咳嗽 。
   (9) 打了針以後她覺得舒服多了 。
   (10) 我們這學期比上學期忙多了 。

第四十七課

2. (1) 帶到　　(2) 作成　　(3) 寫在　　(4) 翻譯成
   (5) 掛在　　(6) 送到　　(7) 交給　　(8) 看作

5. (1) 除了小説以外，魯迅還寫了很多文章。
   (2) 看了這篇文章以後，你有甚麼感想？
   (3) 除了魚以外，別的菜她都愛吃 。
   (4) 青年們的文化生活比以前豐富多了。
   (5) 除了這個故居以外，魯迅在北京還住過三個地方 。
   (6) 這個學院為國家培養了很多大夫。

6. (1) 拉，推到　　(2) 拉到　　　　(3) 拉到
   (4) 推到　　　　(5) 推到，拉到　(6) 拉，推到

第四十八課

2. (1) 院子打掃得很乾淨 。
   (2) 寫着 "恭賀新禧" 四個大字的燈籠掛在門口 。
   (3) 飯菜都準備好了。
   (4) 這件禮物送給了外國阿姨 。

(5) 爆竹都放完了。

(6) 餃子很快包好了。

(7) 李老師寫的春聯貼在門上了 。

(8) 糖，點心 ，茶具都擺好了。

4. (1) 誰見了都喜歡 (2) 哪兒也不想去

(3) 怎麼走也找不到要去的地方

(4) 誰也不想去看 (5) 哪兒也買不到

(6) 甚麼也看不見 (7) 甚麼也沒有

(8) 怎麼找也找不到

6. (1) 桌子上的菜擺得很好看 。

(2) 他們第一次在外國過聖誕節。

(3) 因為他剛參加了球賽， 所以比較累。

(4) 這次考試我們全班同學的成績都很好 。

(5) 她很少生病， 她的身體比較健康 。

(6) 因為春節是全家團聚的節日， 所以他很想家 。

(7) 他甚麼都想學， 可是甚麼都學得不太好。

(8) 這個問題你怎麼回答都可以。

第四十九課

2. (1) 這個電影感動了大家。

(2) 她把這本小說翻譯成法文了。

(3) 小張把小說《李自成》借走了。

(4) 古 波 把帕蘭卡送到北京醫院去了。

(5) 大家把老舍先生叫作 "人民藝術家 " 。

(6) 孩子們把買來的冰棍兒吃完了。

3. (1) 那些活兒被工人們幹完了 。

(2) 我們的行李被同學們拿到宿舍去了。

(3) 小張保持的記錄被古波打破了。

(4) 我的自行車被那位老工人修好了 。

(5) 這位新同學被李老師介紹給大家了。

(6) 魯迅先生被進步青年看作自己的老師 。

4. (1) 常常刮風 (2) 寫了很多話劇

(3) 應該會寫 (4) 關心我們的學習

(5) 外國人也喜歡看 (6) 冬天他也常常去

(7) 古典小說 (8) 頤和園

5. (1) 這是中國最有名的新電影之一 。

(2) 這些工作已經被他們三個人完成了。

(3) 他很少看話劇 ， 連首都劇場在哪兒也不知道 。

(4) 這瓶酒讓他們喝完了。

(5) 他不但見過這位藝術家 ， 而且還跟他談過話 。

(6) 他不但用中文寫信 ， 而且也用中文寫日記。

(7) 這個青年作家的作品非常感動人 。

(8) 那把椅子被我放到院子裡了。

第五十課

個： 代表　鄰居　叔叔　客人　觀眾　青年　湖
　　 司機　學校　茶壺　耳朵　鼻子　本子　月
　　 公園　禮堂　飯館　座位　郵局　窗口　系
　　 問題　建築　廣場　劇場　機會　情況　字
　　 電影　專業　故事　名字　禮物　箱子　球
　　 晚會　話劇　暑假　寒假　假期　學期　詞
　　 小時　星期　信封　牌子　兒子　女兒　碗
　　 售貨員　吸塵器　照像機　留學生　圖書館

張： 畫兒　圖片　郵票　地圖　照片　桌子　床　表

件： 棉襖　襯衫　東西　大衣

條： 馬路　裙子　船　路　腿

套： 茶具　郵票　書　衣服

座： 建築　山　橋　樓

句： 中文　成語　話

本： 小說　雜誌　本子

雙： 筷子　鞋　手

隻： 手　腳　熊貓

4.　(1) 因為 ， 所以　　(2) 雖然 ， 但是　　(3) 要是 ， 就
　　 (4) 除了 ， 還有　　(5) 不但 ， 而且　　(6) 只有 ， 才
5.　(1) 他們是來給老師拜年的 。

　　 (2) 我們全家是今年春節團聚的 。

　　 (3) 醫院外邊停着很多車 。

　　 (4) 他衣服穿得很少 ， 又站在外邊 ， 所以覺得很冷 。

　　 (5) 他是一個偉大的人 ， 又是一個儉樸的人 。

　　 (6) 我們很喜歡這個畫展 ， 李老師也被它吸引住了。

　　 (7) 這個公園沒有意思 ， 連花兒也很少。

(8) 他把這篇課文一句一句地翻譯成法文 。

6.　(1) 他把那封信放在桌子上 。
　　(2) 孩子們聽故事聽得很高興 。
　　(3) 我同學作練習作得很認真 　。
　　(4) 我認識那個人了 。
　　(5) 我們應該幫助他 。
　　(6) 他沒把本子找到 。
　　(7) 我朋友把這本書送給我了。
　　(8) 練習已經作完了 　。
　　(9) 我作得好這件事情。
　　(10) 我沒有被這個話劇感動 　。

APPENDIX B
Texts of Lessons 36-50 in Traditional Characters

第三十六課　　　　這套茶具比那套便宜

帕蘭卡：　古波，我們去百貨大樓，好嗎？我要買茶具。

古波：　　學校旁邊有個商店，為甚麼去百貨大樓呢？

帕蘭卡：　這個商店我去過了，東西不太多。百貨大樓比這個商店
　　　　　大，東西也比這兒多。

古波：　　好吧，我也想去買自行車。
　　　　　（在百貨大樓）

帕蘭卡：　同志，我要一套瓷器茶具。

售貨員：　好，您看看這套，這是江西景德鎮的。

古波：　　景德鎮的瓷器非常有名。

售貨員：　對了。景德鎮生產瓷器的歷史很長了，質量非常好。
　　　　　有人說那兒的瓷器比玉白，比紙薄。

帕蘭卡：　是啊，作得真漂亮！這種茶具一套多少錢？

售貨員：　這套六個茶碗，一共四十二塊二毛八（分）。

帕蘭卡：　有比這個便宜的嗎？

售貨員：　這套唐山的茶具比那套便宜。

古波：　　質量有那套好嗎？

售貨員：　質量也不錯。茶壺沒那個大，只有四個茶碗。唐山瓷
　　　　　生產的歷史沒有景德鎮長，可是解放以後有了很大的
　　　　　發展，質量比以前提高了。

帕蘭卡：　我覺得茶壺上的畫兒比那套畫得好。

售貨員：　這是齊白石的畫兒。茶壺茶碗都好看也很便宜，
　　　　　一共三十塊零四毛。

帕蘭卡：　好，我要這套。

售貨員：　您這是三十二塊，找您一塊六（毛）。

古波：　　請問，買自行車在哪兒？

售貨員：　在外邊，大樓旁邊。

帕蘭卡：　謝謝您。

售貨員：　不謝。

第三十七課　　　這件跟那件一樣長

古波：　　　同志，我看看布中山裝。

售貨員：　　您穿的嗎？給您這件，請到對面試試。

古波：　　　太短了。

售貨員：　　這件比那件大五公分，您再試試。

古波：　　　長短很合適，可是比那件肥得多。

售貨員：　　我給您找一件瘦一點兒的。您看這件，跟那件一樣長，
　　　　　　比那件瘦三公分。

帕蘭卡：　　這件很合適。你穿了中山裝就跟中國人一樣了。

古波：　　　不，鼻子、眼睛還跟中國人不一樣。你看衣服的顏色怎麼樣？

帕蘭卡：　　藍的沒有灰的好看。有灰的嗎？

售貨員：　　有。

古波：　　　好，我要灰的。多少錢一件？

售貨員：　　九塊九毛五。請您到那個窗口交錢。

帕蘭卡：　　同志，有我穿的中式小棉襖嗎？

售貨員：　　有。您要甚麼面兒的？

帕蘭卡：　　我要綢面兒的，上次我在這兒看過。

售貨員：　　綢面兒的現在 還有，您一個星期以後再來看看。
　　　　　　要不，您定作吧，十天就可以了。

古波：　　　買衣服也要下星期來，定作比買祇多三天，還是定作吧。

售貨員：　　作的比買的還要合適一些。您先到三層去看看綢子，
　　　　　　那兒有很多種。

帕蘭卡：　　您看我要買幾米綢子？

售貨員：　　您比我高一點兒，買兩米半吧。

帕蘭卡：　　好，謝謝您。

　　　　　　　*　　　　　*　　　　　*

帕蘭卡：　　啊，五點三刻了。

古波：　　　你的表快五分鐘。

帕蘭卡：　　不早了，快 回學校吧。今天花了不少錢，一共花了一
　　　　　　百零五塊。

古波：　　　我還買了一輛自行車呢，比你多花七十多塊。好，
　　　　　　我現在就騎車回學校。

帕蘭卡：　　你認識路嗎？騎車要注意點兒。

古波：　　　你放心吧。

第三十九課　　　　我們見到了你爸爸、媽媽

丁云：

來信收到了。感謝你對我們的關心。

上星期我和古波去你家。路上我們坐錯了車，我們到你家的時候已經很晚了。我們見到了你爸爸、媽媽。你姐姐也帶着孩子小蘭回家看我們。

你爸爸工作很忙，上月車間里選舉，他當了車間主任。你媽媽説他比以前年輕了。他自己説，這叫〝老驥伏櫪，志在千里〞。我們都沒聽懂。你姐姐告訴我們：〝這是兩句古詩，爸爸的意思是：自己雖然老了，但是還要為實現四個現代化作更多的工作。〞我覺得這句詩很好，就請你姐姐給我寫在本子上了。

你媽媽今年春天已經退休了。她身體很好，現在還能在街道上作一些工作呢。

小蘭真有意思，一看見我，她就指着牆上咱們的照片説：〝啊，照片上的阿姨來了。〞

你們家的鄰居也都非常熱情。前邊的張大爺、對面的李大娘都來看我們，説我們是遠方的客人。

時間很晚了，我和古波要走，你媽媽一定要留我們吃飯。這時候小蘭説話了：〝叔叔、阿姨別走，聽我唱個歌兒。〞她唱了一個《遠方的客人請你留下來》。六歲的小姑娘真聰明！她唱完歌兒，我們真不好意思走了。

跟你家裏人在一起，我和古波都覺得非常愉快。我們要永遠記住這一天。

好了，就寫到這兒吧。希望你常來信。

祝

健康　　　　　　　　　　　　　帕蘭卡　　十二月八日

第四十課　　　運動會

〝運動員排好隊，運動會就要開始了，請運動員排好隊……〞操場上正在廣播。

今天，語言學院大操場真漂亮。主席台上邊寫着〝北京語言學院運動會〞幾個大字，旁邊還有很多彩旗。

帕蘭卡看見古波還坐在那兒，她着急地説：〝古波，你聽到廣播了嗎？怎麼還不去？快去吧。〞

古波是個運動員。冬天，他喜歡滑冰；夏天，他喜歡游泳。

他跑一百米跑得非常快，足球也踢得不錯。帕蘭卡雖然自己不參加比賽，但是，她是一個熱情的觀眾，看比賽的時候她比運動員還激動呢！

　　操場中間，老師們正在打太極拳。帕蘭卡看見李老師也在裏邊，他打得很好，跟他上課一樣認真。打完太極拳，觀眾為他們熱烈地鼓掌。

　　男子一百米已經賽完了。帕蘭卡知道小張跑得也很好，他以前保持了學院男子一百米的記錄。帕蘭卡很想知道今天古波跑得有沒有小張快。這時，又廣播了：

　　〝觀眾請注意：男子一百米第一名古波，十一秒一，打破了張光華十一秒三的院記錄；第二名張光華，十一秒二，也打破了他自己的記錄……〞

　　古波和小張正站在百米的終點那兒。小張高興地對古波說：〝今天你跑得好極了，祝賀你！〞古波也笑着說：〝哪裏，我比你只快0.1秒，這個記錄你一定能打破。〞

第四十一課／四十三課

　　考完試以後，古波和帕蘭卡想好好地玩兒玩兒。他們坐公共汽車到北海公園去。司機告訴他們應該在天安門廣場換車。天安門廣場很大，他們花了十分鐘才穿過去，上了開往北海公園的車。車上很擠，因為到北海公園去的人很多。他們正在公園門口排隊買票的時候，看見同學小張走過來了。古波叫他，可是他沒聽見，走進公園去了。

　　公園裏又有山又有水，美極了。古波一看見山就往上爬，一會兒就爬上去了。從山上能看得很遠，北京的建築都看得清清楚楚。他從山上大聲地喊："帕蘭卡，你也爬上來吧!"帕蘭卡說："我不想上去。這兒有一種黃黃的花兒，真美。你帶照像機來了嗎?快下來給我照一張!"

　　這時候從旁邊走過來一個人，對帕蘭卡說："我給你照吧!"帕蘭卡回過頭來一看，是小張!

　　　　*　　*　　*　　　　　　*　　*　　*
（下午三點多古波和帕蘭卡才從公園走出來。）
帕：　　　我又餓又渴，你呢？
古：　　　我也有點餓了？看，馬路對面有個飯館我們過去吧。
（在飯館裏）
服務員：　請到前邊去，那兒有空桌子。我一會兒就過去。
古：　　　你累了，快坐下來吧。菜單是中文的，你認識的
　　　　　漢字比我多得多，你點菜吧。
帕：　　　很多字我也不認識。服務員給我們送茶來了，請她

給我們介紹介紹吧。
服務員： 我們這兒的小吃比較有名。油餅，炸糕和豆粥都很好吃，豆腐也不錯。
帕： 炸糕是甚麼？
服務員： 炸糕是用牛奶，糖，麵和一些別的東西作的。非常好吃。
古： 好，來兩碗豆粥，一碗豆腐和四個炸糕。
帕： 再來兩個油餅，我們帶回去。

第四十二課　　　愚公移山

　　　古時候有位老人，名字叫愚公，快九十歲了。他家的門口有兩座大山，一家人出來進去很不方便。

　　　一天，愚公對家裏人說：〝這兩座山在咱們家的門口，太不方便了。咱們移走這兩座山，好不好？〞

　　　他的兒子孫子一聽，都說：〝您說得對，咱們明天就開始幹！〞他妻子覺得搬山太難了，她說：〝你們知道這兩座山有多高嗎？這麼大的山你們怎麼搬得動？哪兒放得下這麼多石頭呢？〞

　　　大家說：〝只要我們一起努力幹，就一定搬得了這兩座山。山上的石頭我們可以放到海裏去。〞

　　　第二天，愚公帶着一家人開始搬山了。鄰居有個孩子，聽說要搬山，也高高興興地跟他們一起去了。他們不怕刮風，不怕下雨，夏天不怕熱，冬天不怕冷，每天不停地幹。

　　　有個老人叫智叟，看見愚公一家在搬山，覺得很可笑，就對愚公說：〝你這麼大歲數了，路也走不動了，能搬得動山嗎？〞

　　　愚公回答說：〝你還沒有小孩子聰明！我雖然快要死了，但是我還有兒子，兒子死了，還有孫子。山上的石頭搬走一點兒就少一點兒。我們每天不停地搬，為甚麼搬不走山呢？〞

　　　智叟聽了，沒有話說了。

第四十四課　　　她是跟貿易代表團來的

　　　北京的十一月，天氣一天比一天冷了。古波和帕蘭卡決定星期天再到頤和園去一次。

　　　他們走到頤和園門口的時候，後邊開過來一輛汽車。一個姑娘對着他們喊：〝帕蘭卡！古波！〞帕蘭往車上一看，高興得跳起來：〝達尼亞，你是甚麼時候到中國來的？〞達尼亞從車上走下來說：〝我是十二號到的廣州，昨天剛從上海坐飛機到北

京的。〞

　　〝你是來旅行的嗎？〞

　　〝不，我是跟貿易代表團來的。我們非常忙，只有星期天才有空兒。沒想到在這兒看見你們了，真是太好了。〞

　　〝你第一次到這兒吧？我們給你當向導，怎麼樣？〞

　　他們一起走了進去。帕蘭卡先給這位老同學介紹了一下兒頤和園，她說：〝頤和園是中國有名的古典園林，她是一七五零年開始修建的。第二年是皇帝母親的生日，所以這座山叫萬壽山。前邊的湖就是昆明湖。〞

　　他們來到昆明湖邊達尼亞激動地說：〝這兒又是水，又是山；湖上有橋，有小船；山上有古典建築，風景多麼美啊！〞

　　帕蘭卡跟達尼亞到了長廊，她又介紹說：〝這就是有名的長廊。從東邊到西邊有七百二十八米，上邊畫了一萬四千多幅畫兒，有山水花草，也有人物故事。你看，那是古典小說《三國演義》裏的一個故事。她們正在看畫兒，古波走過來說：〝上山去吧，那兒的畫兒更好看。〞大家爬到山上一看，下邊的昆明湖像鏡子一樣。近的地方可以看到湖邊的亭子、綠樹；遠的地方可以看到藍天下的青山、白塔。這真是一幅又大又美的畫兒啊！

　　太陽下山了，他們才離開頤和園。

第四十五課　　　　看熊貓

　　中國的熊貓是非常珍貴的動物。以前在我們國家看不到，後來中國代表團送了兩隻去。我們的大動物園為這兩位客人修建了一個很漂亮的熊貓館。每天都有很多人去參觀。

　　我和古波來到北京以後，才知道中國人多麼喜歡熊貓啊！這兒的信封、本子、茶具、瓷器、鐘和小孩兒的衣服上常常畫着各種樣子的熊貓。我們還看過介紹熊貓的電影。

　　昨天，我和古波請張光華一起到北京動物園去看熊貓。北京動物園很大，裏邊有幾百種動物，不少是外國朋友送來的。小張指着正在吃草的大象說，它們有的是從南亞來的，有的是從非洲來的。

　　看了大象和獅子以後，我們來到熊貓館。裏邊人多極了，我們擠不進去。小張帶我們到了熊貓館的後邊，那兒有兩隻大熊貓正在吃竹葉。它們的樣子又可愛、又可笑：肥肥的身體，短短的腿，頭非常大，耳朵又這麼小，眼睛上像戴着墨鏡一樣。它們在竹子旁邊不停地走過來走過去。我覺得很奇怪：為甚麼這兒人這麼少？一會兒從屋裏走出來一隻小熊貓。小朋友一看見它，就都跑了過來。有的還喊着：〝麗麗出來了！麗麗出來了！〞小熊貓爬到它媽媽身上，看着給它們照相的人，就像在問：〝我這麼站，照得上嗎？〞真可愛極了。

　　我問旁邊的一個小姑娘，〝麗麗〞是甚麼意思？小姑娘告訴我，麗麗是這個小熊貓的名字。下星期麗麗就要坐飛機出國去了。我又問她：〝你以後就看不見麗麗了，你希望它留在這兒嗎？〞〝希望。可是外國小朋友也希望早點兒看到麗麗啊！〞小姑娘認真地回答。

　　我看着麗麗，心里想：這些熊貓和大象不都是各國人民的友好〝使者〞嗎？

第四十六課/四十七課　　帕蘭卡病了

　　帕蘭卡已經病了兩天了。她覺得很不舒服，頭疼得很厲害，吃不下東西，而且又咳嗽又發燒。昨天下午古波開車把她送到醫院去了。內科大夫檢查了以後，對帕蘭卡説：〝你得了重感冒，要立刻住院。〞護士把她送進內科病房以後，給她打了針，還讓她把大夫開的藥吃下去，那種藥每天要吃六次，每次一片。

　　晚上古波又回到醫院去，帶去了一束花兒，一個錄音機和很多錄音帶。錄音帶上除了西方音樂以外，還有很多好聽的中國民歌。他還帶去了帕蘭卡喜歡吃的炸糕。護士對他説：〝太晚了，你不能進病房去了，病人已經睡覺了。〞她還説：〝除了炸糕以外，別的都可以留下來。我會把這些東西送到她的病房去。〞

　　古波很着急，今天早上一起床就去醫院了。帕蘭卡正躺着聽音樂呢。她一看見古波就把錄音機關上，高興地説：〝我好多了！護士給我量了體溫，已經不發燒了。〞古波笑着説：〝這我就放心了。這幾天天氣不好，得病的人很多。我們班上除了你以外，小張和小李也感冒了。〞

第四十八課/四十九課　　古波的宿舍

　　帕蘭卡好了，古波把她從醫院接回來了。

　　帕蘭卡立刻給媽媽打了一個電話，讓她放心。媽媽説：〝我和你爸爸下個月要來中國看你，你希望我們甚麼時候來？〞帕蘭卡高興地説：〝太好了！你們下個月哪天來都可以。我們快要放暑假了，我和古波每天都有空兒。〞

　　帕蘭卡去古波的宿舍告訴他這個消息的時候，他正在看劇本《茶館》呢。他指 着書説：〝我請你爸爸媽媽看話劇《茶館》吧。這個話劇不但寫得好，而且演得也很成功。誰都説應該看。這是有名的作家老舍寫的，已經翻譯成英文和法文了。現在票還沒賣完，我今天就去買，下個月就買不到了。〞

　　帕蘭卡覺得古波的屋子太亂——地圖和報在地上放 着；茶杯沒有洗，箱子開 着；鞋在書架上擺 着；自行車放在床前邊。她説：〝爸爸媽媽來了以後，一定會來你宿舍看看。你的屋子比誰的都亂……〞

　　古波不好意思地説：〝箱子裏的東西太多了，怎 麼關也關不上。自行車讓我同屋騎坏了，還沒修好呢。地圖叫風從牆上刮下來了……〞

　　帕蘭卡問：〝鞋是不是也被刮到書架上了？〞古波笑 着説：〝好了，好了，我知道你的屋子比我的整齊。你爸爸媽媽來的時候，我一定把屋子打掃乾淨，可是今天我打掃不了一我的吸塵器壞了。〞

第五十課　　　心中的花兒

　　昨天在中國美術館，我參觀了一個畫展。有一幅畫兒，畫的是蘭花，前邊站了很多人，我也走了過去。臨摹這幅畫兒的人真不少，最讓人注意的是一個十二、三歲的小姑娘。她畫得非常認真，一會兒看看那幅畫兒，一會兒在自己的本子上一筆一筆地畫。蘭花很快就畫好了，我和旁邊的人看了都説：〝小姑娘畫得真不錯！〞

　　休息的時候我又見到那個小姑娘，我走過去問她：〝能把你的畫兒給我看看嗎？〞她不好意思地笑了，小聲地對我説：〝畫得不好，請您提提意見吧。〞説 着，把本子給了我。我打開第一頁，上邊貼 着一張周恩來總理的照片。那是周總理逝世前幾天照的，我在很多中國人的家裏都看到過這張照片。第二頁畫了一枝挺立的紅蓮，旁邊還寫着〝周總理逝世一周年〞。我又看第三頁，也是花兒，畫的是風雪中的紅梅。我立刻想到了陳毅的《紅梅》詩。第四頁是迎春花，第五頁、第六頁……都是花兒。最後是她剛畫的蘭花。〝這麼多花兒，你要畫個大花園嗎？〞我問她。小姑娘笑 着説：〝我還沒畫完呢。我不但要畫中國的花兒，還要畫外國的花兒。我要把世界上最美的花兒畫在一起，讓周總理永遠站在花海中微笑。〞

GLOSSARY

(PCR Books I & II, Revised)

Abbreviations

1.	noun	n		8.	adverb	adv
2.	proper noun	prop. n		9.	preposition	prep
3.	pronoun	pron		10.	conjunction	conj
4.	verb	v		11.	particle	ptl
5.	optative verb	opt. v		12.	interjection	int
6.	numeral	num		13.	prefix	pref
7.	measure word	m		14.	suffix	suf

A

阿姨	n	āyí	auntie	39
啊	int	a	*an interjection, oh*	13
啊	ptl	a	*a modal particle*	17
愛	v	ài	to love	45
愛人	n	àirén	spouse, husband or wife	14

B

八	num	bā	eight	11
把	prep	bǎ	a preposition	46
把	num	bǎ	*a measure word*	47
爸爸	n	bàba	father	4
吧	ptl	ba	*a modal particle*	21
白	adj	bái	white	16
百	num	bǎi	hundred	33
擺	v	bǎi	to put; to place	48
百貨大樓	n	bǎihuò dàlóu	department store	36
搬	v	bān	to move; to take away	42
班	n	bān	class	20
半	num	bàn	half	17
辦	v	bàn	to do; to handle; to attend to	28
辦公室	n	bàngōngshì	office	47
幫	v	bāng	to help	22
幫助	v/n	bāngzhù	to help; help	22

薄	adj	báo	thin	36
報	n	bào	newspaper	15
杯	m/n	bēi	*a measure word*, cup	19
北邊	n	běibiān	north; northern part	47
北京	prop. n	Běijīng	Beijing	18
北美洲	prop. n	Běi Měi Zhōu	North America	7
被	prep	bèi	*a preposition*	49
本	m	běn	*a measure word*	15
本	pron	běn	this; one's own; native	34
本子	n	běnzi	notebook	39
鼻子	n	bízi	nose	32
筆	n	bǐ	pen	13
比	prep/v	bǐ	*a preposition showing comparison*, than; to (in a score)	28
比較	adv/v	bǐjiào	comparatively; quite; to compare	4
畢業	v	bìyè	to graduate	44
邊	n	biān	side; edge (of a lake, etc.)	44
遍	m	biàn	*an action measure word, indicating the process of an action from beginning to end*	32
表	n	biǎo	form, table, chart	32
表	n	biǎo	(wrist) watch	35
別	adv	bié	don't	19
別的	pron	biéde	other; another	43
別人	pron	biéren	other people; others	36
冰鞋	n	bīngxié	skates	28
病	v/n	bìng	to be ill; illness	32
病房	n	bìngfáng	ward (of a hospital)	46
病人	n	bìngrén	patient	46
不錯	adj	búcuò	correct; not bad; pretty good	25
不但 ...而且 ...		búdàn...érqiě...	not only ... but also ...	49
不	adv	bù	not; no	3
布	n	bù	cotton cloth	37
不敢當		bù gǎndāng	*(a polite expression in reply to a complement)* I wish I could deserve your compliment. You flatter me.	15
不好意思		bù hǎoyìsi	to feel embarrassed; to find it embarrassing to do sth.	39
不用		bú yòng	there is no need to	31

C

才	adv	cái	only just; not... until...	41
裁判	n/v	cáipàn	referee; to judge	28

菜	n	cài	dish; vegetable	27
菜單	n	càidān	menu	43
參觀	v	cānguān	to visit; to pay a visit	23
參加	v	cānjiā	to take part in; to attend	20
餐廳	n	cāntīng	dining-hall; restaurant	22
草	n	cǎo	grass	44
廁所	n	cèsuǒ	restroom; toilet	10
層	m	céng	*a measure word*, storey, floor	10
茶	n	chá	tea	8
茶館	n	cháguǎn	teahouse	49
茶壺	n	cháhú	teapot	36
茶具	n	chájù	tea set	36
茶碗	n	cháwǎn	teacup	36
差	v	chà	to lack; to be short of	17
常（常）	adv	cháng(cháng)	often	12
嘗	v	cháng	to taste	27
長	adj	cháng	long	31
長城	prop. n	Chángchéng	The Great Wall	32
長短	n	chángduǎn	length	37
唱	v	chàng	to sing	19
唱片	n	chàngpiān	record, disc	19
車	n	chē	vehicle	5
襯衫	n	chènshān	shirt; blouse	16
城	n	chéng	city; town	23
成	v	chéng	to become; to turn into	47
成功	v	chénggōng	to succeed	49
成績	n	chéngjī	result; achievement	35
吃	v	chī	to eat	18
尺	n/m	chǐ	ruler; measurement of length (一尺=1.09 ft)	42
出	v	chū	to come out; to go out	31
出發	v	chūfā	to start out; to set off	23
出院		chū yuàn	to check out from hospital	47
出租汽車		chūzū qìchē	taxi	38
廚房	n	chúfáng	kitchen	22
除了...以外		chúle...yǐwài	besides; except	47
穿	v	chuān	to put on; to wear	16
穿馬路		chuān mǎlù	to cross a street	43
船	n	chuán	boat, ship	44
傳真	n	chuánzhēn	fax	36

99

窗戶	n	chuānghu	window	46
窗口	n	chuāngkǒu	window (for selling ticket, etc.)	34
床	n	chuáng	bed	18
春節	prop. n	Chūn Jié	Spring Festival	48
春天	n	chūntiān	spring	39
詞	n	cí	word	24
詞典	n	cídiǎn	dictionary	11
次	m	cì	*a measure word*, time	31
聰明	adj	cōngming	smart; bright	39
從	prep	cóng	from	16
寸	n/m	cùn	measurement of length (一寸 =1.3 inch)	37
錯	adj	cuò	wrong	38

D

打電話		dǎ diànhuà	to make a phone call	23
打針		dǎ zhēn	to give or receive an injection	46
打錯了		dǎ cuò le	you have dialed the wrong number	23
打開	v	dǎkāi	to open	50
打破	v	dǎpò	to break	40
打掃	v	dǎsǎo	to clean up	48
大	adj	dà	big; large	16
大家	pron	dàjjiā	all; everybody	27
大娘	n	dàniáng	auntie, a respectful address for an elderly woman	38
大聲	adj	dàshēng	in a loud voice; (read, speak, etc.) loudly	34
大使	n	dàshǐ	ambassador	27
大使館	n	dàshǐguǎn	embassy	27
大學	n	dàxué	university; college	31
大洋洲	prop. n	Dàyáng Zhōu	Oceania	7
大爺	n	dàyé	father's elder brother; a respectful form of address for a man older than one's father	3
大衣	n	dàyī	overcoat	16
帶	v	dài	to take (along); to bring (with)	38
戴	v	dài	to wear (cap, glasses, gloves, etc.)	45
代表	n	dàibiǎo	delegate; representative	23
代表團	n	dàibiǎotuán	delegation	23
大夫	n	dàifu	doctor	5
但是	conj	dànshì	but	39
當	v	dāng	to work as; to act as	25
當心	v	dāngxīn	to take care; to look out	43

到	v	dào	to go; to arrive; to reach	27
得病		dé bìng	to fall ill; to contract a disease	32
德國	prop. n	Déguó	Germany	6
的	ptl	de	*a structural particle*	5
得	ptl	de	*a structural particle*	25
地	ptl	de	*a structural particle*	34
燈	n	dēng	lamp; light	48
等	v	děng	to wait	17
第	pref	dì	*a prefix indicating order*	31
弟弟	n	dìdi	younger brother	3
地方	n	dìfang	place	32
地鐵	n	dìtiě	subway	38
地圖	n	dìtú	map	7
地址	n	dìzhǐ	address	20
點	m	diǎn	*a measure word*, o'clock	1
點心	n	diǎnxin	light refreshments; pastry	24
店	n	diàn	shop; store	43
電報	n	diànbào	telegram; cable	34
電車	n	diànchē	trolleybus	38
電話	n	diànhuà	phone call; telephone	23
電腦	n	diànnǎo	computer	22
電視	n	diànshì	TV	23
電影	n	diànyǐng	film; movie	17
電影院	n	diànyǐngyuàn	movie theater	17
釣	v	diào	to fish with a hook and bait	25
頂	m	dǐng	*a measure word*	28
訂	v	dìng	to subscribe to (a newspaper, etc.)	36
丟	v	diū	to lose	41
東邊	n	dōngbiān	east; eastern part	38
冬天	n	dōngtiān	winter	28
東西	n	dōngxi	thing	30
懂	v	dǒng	to understand	24
動物	n	dòngwu	animal	45
動物園	n	dòngwuyuán	zoo	45
都	adv	dōu	all, both	3
豆腐	n	dòufu	bean curd	43
短	adj	duǎn	short	37
鍛煉	v	duànliàn	to do physical training	24
對	adj	duì	right; correct	13
隊	n	duì	team; line	28

對	prep	duì	to; for	39
對不起		duìbuqǐ	(used as an apology) I'm sorry. Excuse me. I beg your pardon.	41
對面	n	duìmiàn	opposite, across the way	22
多	adj	duō	many; much; a lot of	18
多	adv	duō	how	21
多麼	adv	duōme	indicates a high degree, used in an exclamatory sentence, how, what	44
多少	pron	duōshǎo	how many; how much	10

E

餓	v/adj	è	to starve; hungry	43
兒子	n	érzi	son	48
耳朵	n	ěrduo	ear	32
二	num	èr	two	10

F

發燒	v	fā shāo	to have a fever	46
發展	v	fāzhǎn	to develop	36
法國	prop. n	Fǎguó	France	13
法語	n	Fǎyǔ	French	12
翻譯	n/v	fānyi	interpreter; translator; to interpret; to translate	26
飯	n	fàn	meal; cooked rice; food	18
飯館	n	fànguǎn	restaurant	43
方便	adj/v	fāngbiàn	convenient; to make it convenient for	42
方向	n	fāngxiàng	direction	38
房間	n	fángjiān	room	22
房子	n	fángzi	house	22
訪問	v	fǎngwèn	to visit	23
放	v	fàng	to put; to place	34
放假		fàng jià	to have a holiday or vacation	35
放心		fàng xīn	to set one's mind at rest; to be at ease	29
非常	adv	fēicháng	extremely	21
飛機	n	fēijī	airplane	29
非洲	prop. n	Fēi Zhōu	Africa	45
肥	adj	féi	loose-fitting; fat	37
分	m	fēn	a measure word (the smallest Chinese monetary unit)	36
分	m	fēn	a measure word, minute	17
分別	v	fēnbié	to part, be separated from each other	29
分機	n	fēnjī	(of telephone) extension	23

風	n	fēng	wind	33
封	m	fēng	*a measure word*	34
風景	n	fēngjǐng	scenery; landscape	44
夫人	n	fūren	lady; madame; Mrs.	27
服務	v	fúwù	to serve	43
服務員	n	fúwùyuán	waiter; waitress; attendant	19
幅	m	fú	*a measure word*	44
輔導	v	fǔdǎo	to coach, to tutor	20
複習	v	fùxí	to review	23

G

改	v	gǎi	to correct	47
乾杯		gān bēi	to propose a toast; cheers	27
乾淨	adj	gānjing	clean; neat and tidy	48
感動	v	gǎndòng	to move; to touch	49
感冒	v/n	gǎnmào	to catch cold; cold, flu	46
感謝	v	gǎnxiè	to thank, be grateful	21
幹	v	gàn	to work; to do	42
剛	adv	gāng	*indicates the immediate past,* just; only a short while ago	38
高	adj	gāo	tall	37
高興	adj	gāoxìng	glad; happy; delighted	21
告訴	v	gàosu	to tell	14
高速	adj	gāosù	high-speed	39
高速公路	n	gāosù gōnglù	freeway	39
歌兒	n	gēr	song	19
哥哥	n	gēge	elder brother	3
歌劇	n	gējù	opera	26
個	m	ge	*a measure word*	15
各	pron/adv	gè	each; every; various; respectively	43
個子	n	gèzi	height; stature	32
給	prep/v	gěi	to; for; to give	14
跟	prep/v	gēn	with; to follow; to accompany	17
更	adv	gèng	even; still	21
工廠	n	gōngchǎng	factory	23
工程師	n	gōngchéngshī	engineer	14
公分	m	gōngfēn	*a measure word*, centimeter	37
公共	adj	gōnggòng	public	38
公共汽車		gōnggòng qìchē	public bus	38
恭賀新禧		gōnghèxīnxǐ	Happy New Year	48
公斤	m	gōngjīn	kilogram (kg)	42

公路	n	gōnglù	highway	22
公平	adj	gōngping	fair	28
工人	n	gōngren	worker	23
公司	n	gōngsī	company	14
公園	n	gōngyuán	park	33
工作	v/n	gōngzuò	to work; work	14
狗	n	gǒu	dog	22
夠	adj	gòu	enough; sufficient	43
姑娘	n	gūniang	girl	21
古	adj	gǔ	ancient	33
古典	adj	gǔdiǎn	classical	19
鼓掌		gǔ zhǎng	to applaud	40
顧客	n	gùkè	customer	43
故事	n	gùshi	story	38
刮風		guā fēng	(of wind) to blow	33
挂	v	guà	to hang; to put up	34
挂號		guà hào	to register (a letter, etc.)	34
拐彎		guǎi wān	to make a turn, to turn	38
關	v	guān	to close; to shut	46
關上		guānshang	to close; to shut; to turn off	46
關心	v	guānxīn	to care for; to be concerned with	39
觀眾	n	guānzhòng	audience	40
廣播	v	guǎngbō	to broadcast	40
廣場	n	guǎngchǎng	square	41
廣州	prop. n	Guǎngzhōu	*name of a city in southern China*	44
貴	adj	guì	expensive	36
櫃台	n	guìtái	counter	34
貴姓		guì xìng	(polite) May I ask your name?	9
國	n	guó	country; state	6
國際	n	guójì	international	31
國家	n	guójiā	country; state	30
過	v	guò	to live; to get along	30
過	v	guò	to come over; to pass by	41
過	ptl	guo	*a structural particle*	32

H

還	adv	hái	else; in addition; still; to indicate future repetition of an action	15
還是	conj	háishi	or	19
孩子	n	háizi	child	14
海	n	hǎi	sea	50

寒假	n	hánjià	winter vacation	35
喊	v	hǎn	to shout	44
韓國	n	Hánguó	Korea	6
漢語	n	Hànyǔ	Chinese language	15
漢字	n	hànzì	Chinese character	15
航空	n	hángkōng	aviation, air mail	34
好	adj	hǎo	good; well	1
好吃	adj	hǎochī	delicious; tasty	43
好看	adj	hǎokàn	good-looking	21
號	n	hào	number	10
號	n	hào	date; day of the month	20
號碼	n	hàomǎ	number	23
喝	v	hē	to drink	8
和	conj/prep	hé	and; with	13
河	n	hé	river	25
合適	adj	héshì	suitable; fit	37
黑	adj	hēi	black; dark	48
很	adv	hěn	very	2
紅茶	n	hóngchá	black tea	19
紅綠燈	n	hónglǜdēng	traffic light; traffic signal	38
厚	adj	hòu	thick	36
後邊	n	hòubian	back; at the back of; behind	22
後來	n	hòulái	afterwards; later	45
壺	n/m	hú	pot; *a measure word*	36
湖	n	hú	lake	44
護士	n	hùshi	nurse	46
互相	adv	hùxiāng	each other; mutually	15
護照	n	hùzhào	passport	31
花	v	huā	to spend (money, time)	37
花兒	n	huār	flower	21
花茶	n	huāchá	scented tea	19
花園	n	huāyuán	garden	22
滑冰		huá bīng	to skate; skating	28
華僑	n	huáqiáo	overseas Chinese	31
滑雪		huá xuě	to ski; skiing	28
話	n	huà	words; talk; speech	31
畫	v	huà	to paint; to draw	36
畫兒	n	huàr	picture; painting	36
畫報	n	huàbào	illustrated magazine, pictorial	11
話劇	n	huàjù	drama; play	49

壞	adj	huài	bad; broken	49
歡迎	v	huānyíng	to welcome	8
還	v	huán	to return	11
換	v	huàn	to exchange	38
黃	adj/prop. n	huáng	yellow, *a surname*	48
皇帝	n	huángdi	emperor	41
黃河	prop. n	Huáng Hé	the Yellow River	7
灰	adj	huī	grey	37
回	v	huí	to return; to go back	17
回答	v	huídá	to reply; to answer	24
會	optv/v	huì	can; to know how to	26
活	v/adj	huó	to live; alive; living	47
活兒	n	huór	work; job	42
火車	n	huǒchē	train	24
火腿	n	huǒtuǐ	ham	25
貨	n	huò	goods; commodity	36
或者	conj	huòzhě	or	26

			J	
機場	n	jīchǎng	airport	29
雞蛋	n	jīdàn	chicken egg	25
激動	adj	jīdòng	excited	40
機會	n	jīhuì	chance; opportunity	35
...極了		jíle	extremely; exceedingly	40
幾	pron	jǐ	how many; several	15
擠	adj/v	jǐ	crowded; to squeeze	41
寄	v	jì	to mail	34
記	v	jì	to remember; to bear in mind	39
記录	n	jìlù	record	40
家	n	jiā	family; home; house	14
駕駛執照		jiàshǐ zhízhào	driver's license	10
加深	v	jiāshēn	to deepen	26
假期	n	jiàqī	vacation	35
價錢	n	jiàqian	price	36
間	m	jiān	*a measure word*	47
檢查	v/n	jiǎnchá	to check up; inspection	32
件	m	jiàn	*a measure word*	16
見	v	jiàn	to meet; to see	29
健康	adj/n	jiànkāng	healthy; health	27
見面		jiàn miàn	to meet or see each other	29
建築	n/v	jiànzhù	building; to build; to construct	41

106

講	v	jiǎng	to tell; to speak; to explain (a text, etc.)	38
教	v	jiāo	to teach	15
繳	v	jiāo	to pay; hand in; turn over	37
腳	n	jiǎo	foot	41
角	n	jiǎo	*a measure word, a unit of Chinese currency, equals to 1/10 of a kuai/yuan*	36
餃子	n	jiǎozi	dumpling	46
叫	v	jiào	to call; to be called	9
叫	v	jiào	to hire, to call (a taxi, etc.); (in a pivotal sentence) to make, to order	29
叫	prep	jiào	*a preposition*	49
教練	n	jiàoliàn	coach; trainer	25
教室	n	jiàoshì	classroom	15
教授	n	jiàoshòu	professor	13
加州	prop. n	Jiāzhōu	California	10
街	n	jiē	street	38
接(電話)	v	jiē (diànhuà)	to answer (the phone)	23
接(人)	v	jiē (rén)	to meet /pick up (a person)	23
節	n	jié	festival	48
結婚		jiē hūn	to get married	20
節日	n	jiérì	festival; holiday	48
姐姐	n	jiějie	elder sister	14
借	v	jiè	to borrow; to lend	49
介紹	v	jièshào	to introduce	13
今年	n	jīnnián	this year	20
今天	n	jīntiān	today	20
緊	adj	jǐn	close; tight	29
進	v	jìn	to enter; to come in	8
近	adj	jìn	near	44
進步	n/v	jìnbù	progress; advance; to make progress	29
進來		jìn lái	to come in; to enter	26
京劇	n	jīngjù	Beijing opera	16
經歷	n	jīnglì	manager; director	14
九	num	jiǔ	nine	11
酒	n	jiǔ	wine; liquor	27
舊	adj	jiù	old	16
就	adv	jiù	at once; right away	26
橘子	n	júzi	orange	19
橘子水	n	júzishuǐ	orange juice	19
句	m	jù	*a measure word, for sentences*	39

| 覺得 | v | juéde | to think; to feel | 33 |
| 決定 | v/n | juédìng | to decide; to make up (one's mind); decision | 44 |

K

咖啡	n	kāfēi	coffee	17
咖啡館	n	kāfēiguǎn	cafe	17
開	v	kāi	to open	21
開車		kāi chē	to drive a car	23
開會		kāi huì	to hold or to attend a meeting	31
開始	v	kāishǐ	to begin; to start	27
開學		kāi xué	school starts; new term begins	35
看	v	kàn	to see; to look; to read; to watch	7
看(病)	v	kàn (bìng)	(of a patient) to see a doctor, (of a doctor) to treat a patient or an illness	32
考	v	kǎo	to test	35
考試	v/n	kǎoshì	to test; examination	35
科	n	kē	a division of an administrative or academic unit	46
咳嗽	v	késou	to cough	46
渴	adj	kě	thirsty	43
可愛	adj	kěài	adorable; cute; lovely	45
可能	optv/adj	kěnéng	may; probable; possible	46
可是	conj	kěshì	but	26
可笑	adj	kěxiào	funny; ridiculous	45
可以	opt. v	kěyǐ	may	26
刻	m	kè	*a measure word,* quarter (of an hour)	17
課	n/m	kè	class; lesson	17
客氣	adj	kèqi	polite; courteous	8
客人	n	kèren	guest; visitor	39
客廳	n	kètīng	living room	22
課文	n	kèwén	text	23
空兒	n	kòngr	spare time	20
口語	n	kǒuyǔ	spoken language	15
哭	v	kū	to cry; to weep	30
褲子	n	kùzi	pants	16
快	adj	kuài	fast; quick	25
塊	m	kuài	*a measure word, the oral version for "yuan", the basic unit of Chinese currency*	36
筷子	n	kuàizi	chopsticks	27
礦泉水	n	kuàngquánshuǐ	mineral water	25

108

拉	v	lā	to play (string instruments); to pull	31
來	v	lái	to come	13
藍	adj	lán	blue	37
籃球	n	lánqiú	basketball	28
老	adj	lǎo	old; aged	31
姥姥	n	lǎolao	(maternal) grandmother	46
老師	n	lǎoshī	teacher	6
了	ptl	le	*a particle*	13
累	v/adj	lèi	to feel tired, fatigued	43
冷	adj	lěng	cold	33
離	prep	lí	from	30
離開	v	líkāi	to leave	29
李	prop. n	Lǐ	*a surname*	27
邊	n	lǐbiān	inside	22
禮物	n	lǐwù	gift; present	48
理想	adj/n	lǐxiǎng	ideal	26
厲害	adj	lìhai	serious; terrible	46
立刻	adv	lìkè	immediately; at once	46
歷史	n	lìshǐ	history	36
利用	v	lìyòng	to use; to make use of	35
倆	num/m	liǎ	*a numeral-measure word,* two, both	26
連...也..		lián...yě	even	49
練習	n/v	liànxí	exercise; to practice	24
量	v	liáng	to measure	32
涼快	adj	liángkuai	nice and cool; pleasantly cool	33
兩	num	liǎng	two	16
輛	m	liàng	*a measure word (for vehicles)*	37
亮	adj	liàng	light; bright	43
了	v	liǎo	*(as a resultative complement)* to indicate possibility or finality	42
了解	v	liǎojiě	to understand; to know	26
鄰居	n	línjū	neighbour	39
O/零	num	líng	zero	10
零錢	n	língqián	(of money) change; small bills	36
留	v	liú	to remain; to ask somebody to stay	39
流利	adj	liúlì	fluent	25
留學生	n	liúxuéshēng	a student who studies abroad	9
六	num	liù	six	11
樓	n	lóu	storied building; floor	27
路	n	lù	road; way	31

路口	n	lùkǒu	crossing; intersection	38
洛杉磯	prop. n	Luòshāngjī	Los Angeles	10
錄音		lù yīn	to record; recording	46
錄音機	n	lùyīnjī	(tape) recorder	46
旅館	n	lǚguǎn	hotel	41
旅行	v	lǚxíng	to travel	44
綠	adj	lù	green	16
綠茶	n	lùchá	green tea	19
綠燈	n	lùdēng	green traffic light	43
律師	n	lùshī	lawyer	26

M

媽媽	n	māma	mother	4
馬	n	mǎ	horse	38
馬路	n	mǎlù	road; street	38
嗎	ptl	ma	*an interrogative particle*	2
買	v	mǎi	to buy	13
賣	v	mài	to sell	49
慢	adj	màn	slow	25
忙	adj	máng	busy	3
毛	num	máo	*a measure word*, the oral version for "jiao", *a unit of Chinese currency*	36
毛衣	n	máoyī	woolen sweater	37
貿易	n	màoyì	trade	44
帽子	n	màozi	hat; cap	28
沒	adv	méi	not; no; *used to negate the verb* 有	14
沒(有)	adv	méi (you)	not; no; *used to negate past actions*	23
沒關係		méiguānxi	it doesn't matter, that's all right	41
每	pron	měi	every; each	18
美	adj	měi	beautiful	41
美國	prop. n	Měiguó	the United States of America	31
妹妹	n	mèimei	younger sister	14
門	n	mén	door	21
門口	n	ménkǒu	doorway; entrance	41
米	m	mǐ	*a measure word*, meter	37
面包	n	miànbāo	bread	25
秒	m	miǎo	*a measure word*, second (1/60 of a minute)	40
民歌	n	míngē	folk song	19
名	m	míng	*a measure word for people; a measure word*, place (e.g. among winners)	40
明年	n	míngnián	next year	29

明天	n	míngtiān	tomorrow	23
明信片	n	míngxìnpiàn	postcard	34
名字	n	míngzi	name	13
摩托車	n	mótuōchē	motorcycle	41
母親	n	mǔqin	mother	44

N

拿	v	ná	to get; to take	32
哪	pron	nǎ	which	6
哪兒	pron	nǎr	where	10
哪裏	pron	nǎlǐ	*(a polite expression in reply to a compliment)* it's nothing	25
那	pron	nà	that	5
那兒	pron	nàr	there	15
奶酪	n	nǎilào	cheese	25
男	n	nán	male	13
難	adj	nán	difficult	24
南邊	n	nánbiān	south; southern part	38
難過	adj	nánguò	sad	29
南京	prop. n	Nánjīng	*name of a city in China*	34
南美洲	prop. n	Nán Měi Zhōu	South America	7
南亞	prop. n	Nán Yà	South Asia	45
男子	n	nánzǐ	man	40
呢	ptl	ne	*a modal particle*	2
內科	n	nèikē	(of hospital) internal medicine department	32
能	opt. v	néng	can; to be able to	26
你	pron	nǐ	you (sing.)	1
你們	pron	nǐmen	you (pl.)	4
年	n	nián	year	20
新年	n	xīnnián	New Year	48
年輕	adj	niánqīng	young	21
念	v	niàn	to read aloud	24
您	pron	nín	*the polite form of "你"*	8
牛奶	n	niúnǎi	milk	47
農村	n	nóngcūn	countryside; rural areas	24
農民	n	nóngmín	farmer	24
努力	adj	nǔlì	hard-working	29
女	n	nǚ	female	12
女兒	n	nǚ'er	daughter	30
女士	n	nǚshì	*a polite form of address for woman*, lady; madam	9

暖和	adj	nuǎnhuo	nice and warm	33

O

歐洲	prop. n.	Ōu Zhōu	Europe	7

P

爬	v	pá	to climb	44
怕	v	pà	to be afraid; to fear	33
排隊		pái duì	to line up	38
排球	n	páiqiú	volleyball	28
牌子	n	páizi	sign; plate	34
旁邊	n	pángbiān	side	22
胖	adj	pàng	fat	37
跑	v	pǎo	to run	38
朋友	n	péngyou	friend	4
啤酒	n	píjiǔ	beer	19
便宜	adj	piányi	cheap; inexpensive	36
片	m	piàn	*a measure word*, tablets	46
票	n	piào	ticket	16
漂亮	adj	piàoliang	pretty; beautiful	21
乒乓球	n	pīngpāngqiú	table tennis	28
瓶	m	píng	*a measure word*, bottle	19
苹果	n	píngguǒ	apple	19
葡萄	n	pútao	grape	27
葡萄酒	n	pútaojiǔ	grape wine	27

Q

七	num	qī	seven	11
騎	v	qí	to ride (a bicycle, horse, etc.)	37
奇怪	adj	qíguài	to be surprised; strange	35
起	v	qǐ	to get up; to rise	18
起床		qǐ chuáng	to get up (from bed)	18
起飛	v	qǐfēi	(of an airplane) to take off	29
汽車	n	qìchē	automobile; car	38
氣人		qì rén	to enrage somebody, to make somebody upset	28
千	num	qiān	thousand	42
簽証	n	qiānzhèng	visa	28
錢	n	qián	money	35
錢包	n	qiánbāo	purse	42
前邊	n	qiánbiān	front	25
牆	n	qiáng	wall	34

敲	v	qiāo	to knock	33
橋	n	qiáo	bridge	44
親愛	adj	qīn'ài	dear	48
青	adj	qīng	green	44
清楚	adj	qīngchu	clear	41
青年	n	qīngnián	youth	47
晴	adj	qíng	(of weather) fine; clear; sunny	33
情況	n	qíngkuàng	condition; situation; state of affairs	35
請	v	qǐng	please	8
請問	v	qǐngwèn	May I ask...?	9
秋天	n	qiūtiān	autumn	29
球	n	qiú	ball	28
去	v	qù	to go	12
去年	n	qùnián	last year	30
全	adj	quán	whole	48
裙子	n	qúnzi	skirt	16

R

讓	v	ràng	*used in a pivotal sentence*, to let; to ask	19
讓	prep	ràng	*a preposition, used in a passive sentence to introduce the agent*	49
熱	adj	rè	hot	33
熱情	adj	rèqíng	cordial; enthusiastic	30
人	n	rén	person	6
人民	n	rénmín	people	26
人民日報	prop. n	Rénmínrìbào	"the People's Daily" (a newspaper in China)	23
認識	v	rènshi	to know; to be familiar with; to recognize	12
認真	adj	rēnzhēn	conscientious; serious; earnest	24
日	n	rì	date; day of the month	20
日本	prep. n	Rìběn	Japan	21
日記	n	rìjì	diary	49
容易	adj	róngyi	easy	26

S

賽	v/n	sài	to compete; competition; match	28
三	num	sān	three	10
山	n	shān	hill; mountain	41
商店	n	shāngdiàn	shop	13
上	v	shàng	to get on; to get into; to board	29
上次		shàng cì	last time; a previous occasion	37

上課		shàng kè	to attend or to teach a class	17
上班		shàng bān	to go to work; to start working	17
上邊	n	shàngbiān	top; on; over; above	22
上海	prep. n	Shànghǎi	*name of a city in China*	31
上午	n	shàngwǔ	morning	18
上衣	n	shàngyī	upper outer garment; jacket	16
少	adj	shǎo	few; little	22
誰	pron	shéi	who	6
身體	n	shēntǐ	body; health	29
甚麼	pron	shénme	what	7
生	v	shēng	to be born	44
生產	v	shēngchǎn	to produce; to manufacture	36
生詞	n	shēngcí	new word	24
生日	n	shēngri	birthday	20
聖誕節	prep. n	Shèngdàn Jié	Christmas Day	48
詩	n	shī	poem; poetry; verse	33
詩歌	n	shīgē	poem	26
十	num	shí	ten	11
石(頭)	n	shí (tou)	stone; rock	42
時候	n	shíhou	(point of) time	18
時間	n	shíjiān	(duration of) time	31
食堂	n	shítáng	dining-hall	17
實現	v	shíxiàn	to realize; to achieve	31
實驗室	n	shíyànshì	laboratory	15
是	v	shì	to be	4
試	v	shì	to try	27
市	n	shì	city	34
事兒	n	shìr	business; thing	17
世界	n	shìjiè	the world	50
收	v	shōu	to receive	34
收拾	v	shōushi	to put in order; to tidy up	48
收音機	n	shōuyīnjī	radio	34
首	m	shǒu	*a measure word*	33
手	n	shǒu	hand	46
首都	n	shǒudū	capital of a country	31
瘦	adj	shòu	tight; thin; lean	37
售貨員	n	shòuhuòyuán	shop assistant	36
售票處	n	shòupiàochù	ticket office; booking office	41
售票員	n	shòupiàoyuán	ticket seller	38
書	n	shū	book	5

輸	v	shū	to lose	28
書店	n	shūdiàn	bookstore	14
書房	n	shūfáng	study room	22
舒服	adj	shūfu	comfortable; well	46
書架	n	shūjià	bookshelf	39
叔叔	n	shūshu	father's younger brother, uncle	39
暑假	n	shǔjià	summer vacation	35
束	m	shù	*a measure word*, bunch	21
樹	n	shù	tree	33
雙	m	shuāng	*a measure word*, pair	28
水	n	shuǐ	water	19
睡覺		shuì jiào	to go to bed; to sleep	18
說	v	shuō	to speak; to say	13
司機	n	sījī	driver	41
死	v	sǐ	to die	41
四	num	sì	four	10
送	v	sòng	to give as a present; to give	21
送(人)	v	sòng (rén)	to see (or walk) someone home; to see (someone) off	30
宿舍	n	sùshè	dormitory	10
雖然	conj	suīrán	though; although	39
歲	m	suì	*a measure word*, year (age)	20
歲數	n	suìshu	age	42
所以	conj	suǒyǐ	so; therefore; as a result	44

T

他	pron	tā	he; him	3
她	pron	tā	she; her	5
它	pron	tā	it	44
他們	pron	tāmen	they; them	3
她們	pron	tāmen	they; them (for females)	12
它們	pron	tāmen	they (refers to things, animals)	45
太	adv	tài	too; too much	16
太太	n	tàitai	Mrs.; madame	21
太陽	n	tàiyang	the sun	44
談	v	tán	to talk; to chat	26
湯	n	tāng	soup	25
糖	n	táng	sugar	43
躺	v	tǎng	to lie (on one's back)	46
套	m	tào	*a measure word*, set	36
疼	adj	téng	ache; pain; sore	46

踢	v	tī	to kick	28
體溫	n	tǐwēn	(body) temperature	46
體育場	n	tǐyùchǎng	stadium	28
天	n	tiān	day	18
天	n	tiān	sky; heaven	44
天安門	prop. n	Tiān'ānmén	Tiananmen (Gate of Heavenly Peace)	34
天安門廣場	prop. n	Tiān'ānmén Guǎngchǎng	Tiananmen Square	41
天氣	n	tiānqì	weather	31
填	v	tián	to fill	32
條	m	tiáo	*a measure word*	16
條子	n	tiáozi	a short note; a slip of paper	39
跳	v	tiào	to jump	44
跳舞		tiào wǔ	to dance	21
貼	v	tiē	to paste	48
聽	v	tīng	to listen	19
聽説		tīng shuō	it is said that	41
停	v	tíng	to stop; to come to a stop	25
停車	v	tíng chē	to park a car; to stop a car	25
停車場	n	tíngchē chǎng	parking lot	39
同學	n	tóngxué	classmate; schoolmate	20
同志	n	tóngzhì	comrade	31
頭	n	tóu	head	45
頭髮	n	tóufa	hair (on the human head)	32
圖書館	n	túshūguǎn	library	15
推	v	tuī	to push	43
腿	n	tuǐ	leg	45
退休	v	tuìxiū	to retire	39

W

外邊	n	wàibiān	outside	23
外國	n	wàiguó	foreign country	45
外語	n	wàiyǔ	foreign language	9
完	v	wán	to finish; to be over	39
玩兒	v	wánr	to play; to have fun with	23
晚	adj	wǎn	late	25
碗	n/m	wǎn	bowl; *a measure word*, bowl	36
晚飯	n	wǎnfàn	supper; dinner	26
晚上	n	wǎnshang	evening	16
萬	num	wàn	ten thousand	42
王	prop. n	Wáng	*a surname*	15

往	v	wǎng	to go (to a place)	38
網球	n	wǎngqiú	tennis	28
忘	v	wàng	to forget	29
往	prep	wàng	toward; (train, plane, etc.) bound for	38
微笑	v	wēixiào	to smile	50
尾巴	n	wěiba	tail	47
喂	int	wèi	*an interjection,* hello	13
位	m	wèi	*a measure word*	25
為	prep	wèi	for; to	27
胃	n	wèi	stomach	32
為甚麼		wèi shénme	why	34
文化	n	wénhuà	culture	27
文學	n	wénxué	literature	26
問	v	wèn	to ask	9
問題	n	wèntí	question; problem	18
我	pron	wǒ	I; me	2
我們	pron	wǒmen	we; us	6
臥室	n	wòshì	bedroom	22
屋(子)	n	wū(zi)	room	48
五	num	wǔ	five	10
午飯	n	wǔfàn	lunch	28
舞會	n	wǔhuì	dance; ball	20

X

西邊	n	xībiān	west; western part	41
吸塵器	n	xīchénqì	vacuum cleaner	48
希望	v/n	xīwàng	to hope; to wish; hope; wish	31
吸煙		xī yān	to smoke	8
西裝	n	xīzhuāng	Western-style clothes	37
習慣	v/n	xíguàn	to be used to; to be accustomed to; habit; custom	33
洗	v	xǐ	to wash	41
喜歡	v	xǐhuan	to like; to be fond of	19
洗澡		xǐ zǎo	to take a bath	22
洗澡間	n	xǐzǎojiān	bathroom	22
系	n	xì	department (in a college)	15
下	v	xià	to get off (bus, plane, etc.)	38
下課		xià kè	class is over or dismissed	17
下	n	xià	*used before a noun or a measure word to indicate coming later in time or order,* next	37
下(雨)	v	xià (yǔ)	to fall (It's raining)	33

117

下班		xià bān	to get off work	17
下邊	n	xiàbiān	below; under; underneath	34
夏天	n	xiàtiān	summer	29
下午	n	xiàwǔ	afternoon	18
先	adv	xiān	first	32
先生	n	xiānsheng	Mr.; sir; gentleman	12
現代	n	xiàndài	modern	19
現在	n	xiànzài	now; nowadays	11
香蕉	n	xiāngjiāo	banana	19
箱子	n	xiāngzi	suitcase	28
想	v/opt. v	xiǎng	to want; to think; to miss	14
像	v	xiàng	to be like; to resemble; to take after	21
向導	n	xiàngdǎo	guide	41
小	adj	xiǎo	little; small	22
小吃	n	xiǎochī	snack	43
小吃店	n	xiǎochīdiàn	snack bar	43
小姐	n	xiǎojie	Miss; young lady	19
小聲	adj	xiǎoshēng	in a low voice	46
小時	n	xiǎoshí	hour	31
小説	n	xiǎoshuō	novel; short story	41
小提琴	n	xiǎotíqín	violin	31
小學生	n	xiǎoxuésheng	elementary school student	27
笑	v	xiào	to laugh; to smile	30
些	m	xiē	*a measure word*, some	24
鞋	n	xié	shoes	28
寫	v	xiě	to write	14
謝謝	v	xièxie	to thank	8
新	adj	xīn	new	15
心	n	xīn	heart	30
辛苦	adj	xīnku	hard working; with much toil	31
新年	n	xīnnián	New Year	48
新聞	n	xīnwén	news	23
信	n	xìn	letter	14
信封	n	xìnfēng	envelope	34
信箱	n	xìnxiāng	P.O. Box; letter box; mail box	
星期	n	xīngqī	week	20
星期日(天)	n	xīngqīrì (tiān)	Sunday	20
行李	n	xíngli	luggage; baggage	28
姓	v/n	xìng	(one's) surname is ...; surname	9
姓名	n	xìngmíng	full name; surname and given name	34

修	v	xiū	to build (road, bridge, etc.); to repair	38
休息	v	xiūxi	to rest; to take a break	18
學	v	xué	to study; to learn	9
學期	n	xuéqī	term; semester	35
學生	n	xuésheng	student	9
學習	v	xuéxí	to study; to learn	9
學校	n	xuéxiào	school	31
學院	n	xuéyuàn	college; institute	9
雪	n	xuě	snow	33
		Y		
亞洲	prop. n	Yà Zhōu	Asia	45
研究	v	yánjiū	to research	26
顏色	n	yánsè	color	37
演	v	yǎn	to perform; to play; to act	49
眼睛	n	yǎnjing	eye	32
眼鏡	n	yǎnjìng	glasses	16
演員	n	yǎnyuán	actor/actress; performer	49
要	v/opt. v	yào	to want; to wish to; must	19
要	adv	yào	will; to be going to	29
藥	n	yào	medicine	46
要是	conj	yàoshi	if	41
爺爺	n	yéye	grandpa	42
也	adv	yě	also; too	2
頁	n/m	yè	page; *a measure word*, page	50
葉子	n	yèzi	leaf	33
一	num	yī	one	10
衣服	n	yīfu	clothes; clothing	37
一 ... 就 ...		yī...jiù...	no sooner ...than ...; as soon as	39
醫院	n	yīyuàn	hospital	46
一定	adv/adj	yídìng	definitely; certainly	20
一共	adv	yígòng	altogether; in all	36
一會兒	n	yíhuìr	a little while	41
一路平安		yílùpíng'ān	to have a nice trip	29
一下兒		yíxiàr	a little while	11
一樣	adj	yíyàng	same; identical	37
以後	n	yǐhòu	after; in the future; afterwards	17
已經	adv	yǐjing	already	31
以前	n	yǐqián	before; in the past; previously	32
椅子	n	yǐzi	chair	22
一點兒		yìdiǎnr	a little; a bit	25

意見	n	yìjiàn	criticism; comments or suggestions	43
一起	adv/n	yìqǐ	together	17
意思	n	yìsi	meaning	39
陰天	n	yīntiān	cloudy day	33
因為	conj	yīnwèi	because	48
音樂	n	yīnyuè	music	19
音樂會	n	yīnyuèhuì	concert	20
銀行	n	yínháng	bank	14
應該	opt. v	yīnggāi	should; ought to	26
英國	prop. n	Yīngguó	Britain	13
英語	n	Yīngyǔ	English	12
贏	v	yíng	to win	28
營業員	n	yíngyèyuán	shop assistant	34
永遠	adv	yǒngyuǎn	always; forever	39
用	v	yòng	to use; to make use of	11
油餅	n	yóubǐng	deep-fried pancake	43
郵局	n	yóujú	post office	34
郵票	n	yóupiào	stamp	34
游泳		yóu yǒng	to swim; swimming	25
有	v	yǒu	to have; there be	14
有的	pron	yǒude	some	34
有(一)點兒		yǒu (yi) diǎnr	a bit	43
友好	adj	yǒuhǎo	friendly	23
有名	adj	yǒumíng	famous; well-known	26
有時候		yǒu shíhou	sometimes	18
友誼	n	yǒuyì	friendship	27
有意思		yǒu yìsi	interesting	20
又	adv	yòu	again; in addition to; more	27
右邊	n	yòubiān	right	22
魚	n	yú	fish	25
愉快	adj	yúkuài	happy; delighted	39
雨	n	yǔ	rain	33
語法	n	yǔfǎ	grammar	15
雨傘	n	yǔsǎn	umbrella	11
語言	n	yǔyán	language	31
雨衣	n	yǔyī	raincoat	37
預報	v	yùbào	forecast	33
圓	m	yuán	*a measure word, the basic unit of Chinese currency*	36
遠	adj	yuǎn	far; distant	30

遠方	n	yuǎnfāng	distant place	39
願意	opt. v	yuànyì	to be willing to	29
院子	n	yuànzi	courtyard, yard	47
約會	n	yuēhuì	appointment	20
月	n	yuè	month	20
閱覽室	n	yuèlǎnshì	reading-room	15
運動	v/n	yùndòng	to exercise (oneself); sports	40
運動會	n	yùndònghuì	sports meet	40
運動員	n	yùndòngyuán	athlete	40

Z

雜誌	n	zázhì	magazine	15
在	v/prep	zài	to be at /in/ on a place	10
再	adv	zài	again; once more	25
再見	v	zàijiàn	good-bye	11
早	adj	zǎo	early	26
早飯	n	zǎofàn	breakfast	28
怎麼	pron	zěnme	how; why	38
怎麼樣	pron	zěnmeyàng	how, usu. used as a predicate or complement	22
炸糕	n	zhágāo	fried cake	43
站	v	zhàn	to stand	29
站	n	zhàn	(bus, train) stop	38
占線		zhàn xiàn	the (phone) line is busy	23
張	m/prop. n	zhāng	*a measure word*, piece; a surname	16
招待會	n	zhāodàihuì	reception	27
着急		zháo jí	to feel anxious, be worried	35
找	v	zhǎo	to look for; to find;	16
找錢		zhǎo qián	to give change, to return the balance of money	36
趙	prop. n	Zhào	a surname	31
照片	n	zhàopiàn	photograph	23
照像		zhào xiàng	to take a picture; to have one's photograph taken	29
照像機	n	zhàoxiàngjī	camera	41
這	pron	zhè	this	4
這麼	pron	zhème	so; such	42
這樣	pron	zhèyàng	so; such; like this	32
着	ptl	zhe	*a particle*	34
這兒	pron	zhèr	here	16
真	adj	zhēn	real; true; genuine	21

針	n	zhēn	injection; needle	46
整理	v	zhěnglǐ	to put in order; to straighten out; to arrange	22
整齊	adj	zhěngqí	neat; tidy	48
掙	v	zhèng	to earn , to make (money)	35
正常	adj	zhèngcháng	normal; regular	32
正在	adv	zhèngzài	*an adverb indicating an action in progress*	23
只	m	zhī	*a measure word*	45
枝	m	zhī	*a measure word*	50
知道	v	zhīdao	to know	20
職員	n	zhíyuán	office worker; staff member	14
紙	n	zhǐ	paper	13
指	v	zhǐ	to point at; to point to	34
只	adv	zhǐ	only	36
只有	conj	zhǐyǒu	only *(indicates a necessary condition, usu. used with 才)*	44
鐘	n	zhōng	clock	31
終點	n	zhōngdiǎn	terminal point; destination	38
中國	prop. n	Zhōngguó	China	6
中間	n	zhōngjiān	center; middle	42
中式	n	zhōngshì	Chinese style	37
中文	n	Zhōngwén	Chinese language	15
種	m	zhǒng	*a measure word*, kind; type; sort	36
重	adj	zhòng	heavy	42
種	v	zhòng	to grow; to plant	46
粥	n	zhōu	porridge	43
住	v	zhù	to live, to reside	10
祝	v	zhù	to wish	21
祝賀	v/n	zhùhè	to congratulate; congratulation	20
注意	v	zhùyì	to pay attention to	29
住院		zhù yuàn	to be hospitalized	46
專業	n	zhuānyè	specialty; profession; major	35
準備	v	zhǔnbèi	to prepare	25
桌子	n	zhuōzi	table	22
字	n	zì	character, word	15
自己	pron	zìjǐ	self	30
自行車	n	zìxíngchē	bicycle	36
總(是)	adv	zǒng(shi)	always	22
走	v	zǒu	to go; to walk	17
足球	n	zúqiú	soccer	28

122

嘴	n	zuǐ	mouth	32
最	adv	zuì	*indicates the superlative degree*	33
最後	n	zuìhòu	last	50
最近	n	zuìjìn	recently; lately	32
昨天	n	zuótiān	yesterday	28
左邊	n	zuǒbiān	left side	32
坐	v	zuò	to sit; to take a seat	10
作	v	zuò	to do	14
座	m	zuò	*a measure word*	44
作家	n	zuòjiā	writer	26
座位	n	zuòwei	seat	38